Liberating Scripture

Studies in Missional Hermeneutics, Theology, and Praxis

The volumes in this series explore the significance of the so-called "missional turn" for Christian hermeneutics, theological reflection, and praxis. This entails both a critical reconstruction of mission in more holistic and decolonizing terms, as well as the ways in which this renewed conception of mission reorients biblical interpretation, theological reflection, and Christian praxis. In so doing, the series seeks to explore and reimagine texts and themes, hermeneutical dynamics, theological issues, and faithful, located engagement for a post-Christendom church in the contemporary world.

Liberating Scripture

An Invitation to Missional Hermeneutics

BY

Michael Barram

AND

John R. Franke

FOREWORD BY

Drew G. I. Hart

AFTERWORD BY

Lisa M. Bowens

CASCADE *Books* · Eugene, Oregon

LIBERATING SCRIPTURE
An Invitation to Missional Hermeneutics

Studies in Missional Hermeneutics, Theology, and Praxis

Cascade Books
An Imprint of Wipf and Stock Publishers
199 W. 8th Ave., Suite 3
Eugene, OR 97401

www.wipfandstock.com

PAPERBACK ISBN: 978-1-6667-0257-6
HARDCOVER ISBN: 978-1-6667-0258-3
EBOOK ISBN: 978-1-6667-0259-0

Cataloguing-in-Publication data:

Names: Barram, Michael D., 1966– [author]. | Franke, John R. [author]. | Hart, Drew G. I.
[foreword writer]. | Bowens, Lisa M. [afterword writer].

Title: Liberating Scripture : an invitation to missional hermeneutics / by Michael Barram
and John R. Franke ; foreword by Drew G. I. Hart ; afterword by Lisa M. Bowens.

Description: Eugene, OR: Cascade Books, 2024 | Series: Studies in Missional Hermeneu-
tics, Theology, and Praxis | Includes bibliographical references and index.

Identifiers: ISBN 978-1-6667-0257-6 (paperback) | ISBN 978-1-6667-0258-3 (hardcover) |
ISBN 978-1-6667-0259-0 (ebook)

Subjects: LCSH: Missions—Theory—Biblical teaching. | Bible—Hermeneutics. | Mis-
sions—Theory. | Missions—Biblical teaching.

Classification: BV2073 B37 2024 (paperback) | BV2073 (ebook)

VERSION NUMBER 03/05/24

For Jim Brownson

visionary pioneer of missional hermeneutics

Contents

Foreword

By Drew G. I. Hart

DEAR READERS, IF SOMEONE had told me ten years ago that I would be writing the foreword for a book about missional hermeneutics, I would have laughed in disbelief. Such a response would be because of my sustained skepticism about any language related to "mission," due to its inherent colonial roots and damaging legacy that continues to do real harm to this very day. Mission logics have emerged out of Western Christendom's colonial pursuits, which have oppressed and harmed so many peoples all around the world. So, there is a real irony in writing this foreword—precisely because I have had multiple conversations with John Franke and Michael Barram, who are both dear friends, about my trouble with "missional" anything.

It's this very irony that sets the stage for my foreword. I am aware that missional theology and hermeneutics have sought to reframe mission away from the colonizing "missions" minded projects of the past and turn our attentiveness and participation towards the mission of God in creation. I studied missional theology with John Franke and appreciate these interventions. And yet, my persisting reservations about the term "missional" are still rooted in a profound concern about its ongoing entanglements with colonialism. I haven't been convinced that missional theology and hermeneutics are capable of breaking from the legacy of Christendom and colonizing Christianity. And it doesn't take much effort to see how the inertia of colonialism continues to sweep up popular usages of missional projects today. Many "missions" projects have been rebranded as missional, with very little embodied difference on the ground. The history of mission, given its overlaps with the deep legacy of colonialism, is a history that the church must grapple with honestly. It has been too easy for white and/or Western-ized Christians to conflate their culture and ways of life with the gospel and to impose paternalistic, hierarchical, racist, and colonizing practices onto other people groups as the one universal way, in the name of mission. In the end, many people end up embodying an oppressive gospel, calling it God's work, while being little more than bad news to the least, last, and little ones Jesus stands with. I've witnessed how the logics of mission have frequently been caught up by a "diseased social imagination," as so eloquently described by Willie James Jennings. And yet, it is precisely this problem with "mis-sion" within Western Christianity that John Franke and Michael Barram argue necessitates direct engagement. They call for a radical reimagining of mission that is severed from its colonial past, and a reorientation towards God's liberating mission and purpose.

I have gone back and forth with John and Michael in lively dialogue on this subject. They have insisted to me that Christendom and the coloniz-ing logics tucked into "mission" must be intentionally engaged at the root, through scriptural and theological reasoning that make visible God's activity and purpose in the world. This is a compelling argument. Basically, they are saying that the language of mission must be interrogated and re-centered around God's holistic purposes revealed in Scripture; otherwise, the inertia of "missions" ideology will persist. In my back-and-forth conversations with them, I usually concede, albeit with a measured reservation, that "missional" can indeed be a meaningful intervention, if—and only if—it carries the sub-versive vocation of a deliberately decolonizing and liberating ethic of God. It is a concession made with the understanding that without this commitment, the tide of colonialism and white supremacy threatens to overwhelm even the most insightful missional scholarship.

That is where we find common ground and overlaps in concerns. We all agree that mission must be severed from its colonizing roots and, if mission language is still to be employed, it must be reimagined as discern-ing and enacting God's liberating purposes disclosed in Scripture. On that point we all concur.

So, my thinking has softened a little through ongoing dialogue with John Franke and Michael Barram. I respect their hearts, their commitments, and their ultimate goals. Although I still have some reservations, I have come to better understand their vision for recasting missional language and hermeneutics in liberative terms that reflect the purposes of God.

And so, we find ourselves at this moment, with me, of all people, penning a foreword for a book on missional hermeneutics. Why? Because John and Michael have succeeded. In *Liberating Scripture* they have charted a course for missional hermeneutics and theology that boldly discerns and actively engages in God's liberating mission and purposes. This work represents a vital step forward for the field, a clarion call for a more intentional and transformative engagement with Scripture.

In the pages that follow, John and Michael present a compelling thesis—a vision of missional hermeneutics that not only reads scripture from the perspective of God's mission but also liberates both Scripture and its readers from the shackles of problematic interpretations. They invite us to embark on a journey that encompasses the triune God's eternal mission of love, God's mission to liberate creation, and the church's pivotal role in embodying and proclaiming God's reign.

This book isn't just scholarly research; it is a call to actively participate in God's justice and liberation. It gestures us to engage in a missional hermeneutic that dismantles oppressive structures and brings forth a more inclusive and just kingdom where everyone is safe and everyone has enough. The book seamlessly intertwines postmodern philosophy, contextual hermeneutics, and a reverence for the diverse voices within Scripture. It fosters humility in biblical interpretation, recognizing that the mystery of God can never be fully contained within our finite understanding. In the end, what John and Michael have achieved in *Liberating Scripture* is nothing short of a milestone moment for a church in desperate need of transformation. This book is not merely an intellectual exercise, it is a call to embody the liberating mission of God in a world yearning for justice and healing.

As a co-host of InVerse Podcast, I, along with my friend and colleague Jarrod McKenna, have routinely asked guests to tell stories about their memories and encounters with the Bible. And then we explicitly ask them whether they experienced the Bible as liberating or oppressive in their lives. We ask this because we understand that interpretations of the Bible have been used for healing and for harm. Our readings need to be decolonized. The Bible has been both a tool of oppression and a sacred text of liberation, depending on how it is wielded or held. But the deepest stream within holy

Scripture, fulfilled in the person of Jesus Christ, flows in the direction of God's liberating love and joy-filled justice.

From Moses to Miriam, from the prophets to the psalmists, from Mary's Magnificat to Jesus's manifesto in Luke 4, the message is clear: the last shall be first and the first shall be last. The proud are brought down and the lowly are lifted up. The mighty are cast off their thrones while the hungry are filled with good things. This is the liberating mission of God, especially revealed in Jesus, echoing through Scripture from Genesis to Revelation.

John and Michael are two of the most insightful minds around when it comes to missional hermeneutics and theology. In this book, they lay out a thoughtful proposal for reading Scripture in participatory and liberatory ways that reflect God's purposes. While there is more work to be done, this book represents an important step in the right direction for missional reasoning. I am convinced that my friends have put forth a vision of missional hermeneutics and theology that can help liberate both Scripture and its readers for Jesus-shaped action in the world. May their work inspire the church towards greater faithfulness and participation in the "mission" (wink) of God.

Preface

IN 1998, THE LANDMARK volume *Missional Church: A Vision for the Sending of the Church in North America* was published by a group of scholars connected to the newly formed *Gospel and Our Culture Network*. The authors argued that the church is called to move from being a church with a mission component to being a fully missional church. The book had such a significant effect that the word *missional*, a term seldom used before its publication, has since become a commonplace not only in the lexicon of the North American church, but the global church as well. Individuals, churches, denominations, and schools have appropriated missional language—some of them in ways that are at odds with what the authors of *Missional Church* intended—and have made it a standard bearer for wide variety of programs and activities.

Later in the same year, James Brownson, a New Testament scholar and original participant in the *Gospel and Our Culture Network*, published the less well-known work, *Speaking the Truth in Love: New Testament Resources for a Missional Hermeneutic*. In this volume, as near as we can tell, Brownson both coined the term *missional hermeneutic* and gave early expression to some of its distinguishing features. He raised a critical interpretive question: if the church is called to move from being a church with a mission component to being a fully missional church—that is, to become a community in which the missional purposes of God in the world are central to all that the church is and does, what are implications of this shift for hermeneutics?

Hermeneutics is the branch of knowledge that deals with interpretation and is particularly associated with the interpretation of the Bible and other literary texts. While Brownson's book explicitly focused on the interpretation of biblical texts from a missional perspective, it implicitly raised larger questions of interpretation related to theology, philosophy, history, and ministerial praxis, especially from the perspective of Christian faith communities.

In 2002, at the annual meeting of the Society of Biblical Literature, Brownson delivered the keynote address for the inaugural meeting of what would eventually become the Forum on Missional Hermeneutics, a group that has convened annually since then to explore and wrestle with questions of hermeneutics, or interpretation, from a missional perspective. For those who are interested, we briefly tell the story of that group and list all of our sessions to date in an appendix to this volume. The two of us have been co-chairing the Forum together for over a decade now, leading a gifted steering committee of scholars and practitioners. In that role, we believe that the time is ripe for an introduction to missional hermeneutics that both draws on the contributions to this conversation over the past twenty plus years, and charts a course for further engagement and research in this emerging discipline.

While we hope this volume serves as a helpful introduction, we intend it more as an invitation to an ongoing conversation that we believe, by its very nature, must be characterized by both plurality and pluralism. No single person or community is able to define and fully explicate the field of missional hermeneutics because it seeks to be faithful to the mission of God in the world. These good purposes extend to all people, from every tribe, nationality, ethnicity, gender, and socioeconomic class. As such, all people have a stake in this conversation and are invited to participate in it. It is our hope that this volume may prove to be useful in a variety of settings, including private study, local church groups, neighborhood gatherings, as well as in college and seminary classrooms.

As the authors of this volume, we are only too well aware of the limitations of our own perspectives and backgrounds. Both of us are white, middle-class, heterosexual males who have seminary and doctoral degrees. Both of us teach in institutions of higher learning, worship and serve in leadership in well-established mainline Presbyterian churches, and have the time and resources to engage in research and writing as well as travel to academic conferences to interact and confer with other colleagues. In short, we live privileged lives that allow us to collaborate on a project like this and the series that will flow from it.

We are aware that the very privilege that enables us to launch this project also limits our ability to perceive many of the issues and perspectives that are central to it. In that spirit, we offer this book as a welcoming invitation to wider dialogue and discussion—in the hope that it will serve as a catalyst for scriptural interpretation leading to more faithful participation in the dream of God for creation, a world where everyone has enough and no one needs to be afraid.

Acknowledgments

Michael

I am grateful to Saint Mary's College of California for supporting the research and writing of this book. Colleagues in the Department of Theology & Religious Studies, the Offices of the Dean of the School of Liberal Arts and the Provost, and the Office of Faculty Development have helped to provide me the space and funding for conference presentations, writing retreats, and a recent sabbatical. I would also like to thank the First Presbyterian Church of Berkeley for sponsoring a five-week adult course on missional hermeneutics in the fall of 2023 that enabled me to explore some of the ideas and practices detailed in this book with the great folks there. Finally, I want to express my love and appreciation for my adult daughters, Jordan and Devyn, and to Kelli, my love, best friend, and confidant. The three of you teach me, sustain me, and inspire me. My "one wild and precious life" (as Mary Oliver put it so eloquently) is immeasurably richer and fun because I get to share it with each of you. I love each of you so much!

John

I would like to thank the congregation, session, and staff of Second Presbyterian Church in Indianapolis for their generous support of my teaching and writing as their theologian in residence. I am grateful to be part of a community shaped by dedicated participation in the mission of God coupled with a genuine commitment to excellence, integrity, and collegiality. We also have a lot of fun together! Thanks to everyone—congregants, volunteers, and staff members—for making it a pleasure to get up in the morning and go to work. I also thank the participants in my classes at the church as well as my students at Christian Theological Seminary, Fuller Theological Seminary, and Princeton Theological Seminary for their patient listening and thoughtful interaction with the ideas developed here. They have helped make this a better book than it would have been. Finally, I would like to thank my wife, Linda Dietch, who makes coming home from work a joy. I love you!

As you join the two of us in this conversation, we readily acknowledge that our contributions in this book draw on the intellectual curiosity and deep collegiality of the many folks whose efforts and voices have shaped the interpretive posture we introduce in these pages. In addition to those we have already mentioned, we would especially like to honor and express our gratitude to the members of the steering committee of the Forum on Missional Hermeneutics, past and present (see the appendix at the back of the book). These valued colleagues have theorized, explored, assessed, and fostered the development of missional hermeneutics, and we sincerely hope that they find in *Liberating Scripture* a fitting tribute to their many significant contributions to our missional hermeneutics conversations. We are especially grateful to colleagues and friends Michael J. Gorman, Greg McKinzie, and Drew G. I. Hart, each of whom read and provided helpful feedback on earlier drafts of this work. We would also like to thank Amy-Jill Levine for generously providing critical feedback on an earlier draft. Of course, we take responsibility for the final form of the book.

In the end, we want to express particular appreciation for our esteemed mentor in this work, Jim Brownson, whose pioneering and prescient vision for a "missional hermeneutic" inspired this interpretive movement that now continues into a third decade. Biblically and theologically astute, argumentatively precise, and rhetorically brilliant, Jim pointed out the missional path that many of us would continue to travel, and it is to him that we humbly and gratefully dedicate this book.

Introduction

THE TITLE OF THIS book, *Liberating Scripture*, is purposefully intended as a double entendre. On the one hand, reading and engaging with the Bible can, of course, be an illuminating and deeply liberating experience. On the other hand, we have a tendency as humans to shackle Scripture, even if unintentionally, within a range of interpretive assumptions and perspectives that can undermine and hinder its liberative power. Therefore, the Bible often needs to be liberated *from us* even as it offers liberation *for us*. Both facets of this double entendre—*liberating Scripture*—are significant for what we are seeking to accomplish in this book.

We have two primary goals as we write. The first is to invite our readers into an approach to biblical interpretation that has become known as "missional hermeneutics," a fresh interpretive posture that we believe can help to illuminate Scripture's liberative function in and for our lives, even as it can assist in liberating the Bible itself from the ways in which we often shackle it within problematic interpretive assumptions and perspectives. Missional hermeneutics suggests that we read and interpret Scripture most appropriately, responsibly, and faithfully from the perspective of its witness to who God is, what God cares about, and what God is doing in and throughout the created order. In short, a missional approach to biblical interpretation invites us to read Scripture from the perspective of the purposes—what we call the "mission"—of God.

We are convinced that the "missional" approach to reading and interpreting the Bible that we describe in these pages makes a significant difference in how we as readers interact with, understand, and are shaped by Scripture. As two of the leading voices in the development of missional hermeneutics, we have written this book to introduce you, our readers, to this interpretive approach, inviting you to join us in exploring and engaging with it. While this emerging subfield of biblical interpretation does not represent an entirely new methodology for reading and studying the Bible, it does provide what we find to be a helpful and significant framework within which to interpret biblical texts responsibly, insightfully, and faithfully. In short, this book serves as an invitation to participate in a powerful and nuanced approach to biblical interpretation that really can make a difference in how we read and make sense of Scripture.

Our second goal, one to which we will turn in the second part of the book, is to offer a new and constructive proposal for an explicitly liberative missional hermeneutics that, for us, even more fully reflects and fosters the two-directional scriptural liberation suggested by the book's title, *Liberating Scripture*. In proposing a *particular* vision for missional hermeneutics going forward, we acknowledge our indebtedness to many fascinating and generative missional hermeneutics conversations among esteemed colleagues and friends that we have had the privilege to participate in over the past two decades—even as we intentionally seek to move the conversation further.

We begin in part 1 with a basic introduction—really, an invitation—to missional hermeneutics. Chapter 1 examines what we and our colleagues mean by the term "missional," and why it matters. Chapter 2 turns to matters of interpretation—what scholars often call "hermeneutics"—exploring how a "missional" lens relates to and can enhance biblical interpretation, specifically. As we summarize and analyze this missional interpretive movement, we seek to do so in a way that accurately captures its fundamental dynamics and implications. Indeed, we hope that our many missional hermeneutics conversation partners will find that these chapters accurately and appropriately reflect the primary considerations and concerns that have been voiced over the years, even if we haven't always cited writings or writers explicitly.

In part 2, we attempt to offer a constructive proposal for a particular way of construing and engaging in missional hermeneutics going forward. While our approach consciously and intentionally builds upon previous trajectories within missional interpretation, it moves into some new territory as we attempt to take seriously certain challenges and opportunities characteristic of postmodern realities. Our particular nuancing of missional hermeneutics in this second part of the book reflects and reveals much about our personal and professional journeys. That is, our perspective in this second part of the book has a lot to do with our own life experiences, as we have wrestled with matters of faith and how to make sense of the Bible—and as we seek to participate actively and faithfully in God's unfolding mission, especially as illuminated in Jesus of Nazareth. At the same time, our approach attempts to draw together various strands of our intellectual and disciplinary inter-ests, ponderings, and concerns as biblical scholar (Michael) and theologian (John). While our readers may not resonate with everything we put forward in these pages, we humbly and yet boldly offer this proposal as a vision for missional biblical interpretation that has so far proven to be liberative in our own lives and journeys of faith. At the very least, we hope that it will serve to inspire deeper and wider discussion about and engagement with missional hermeneutics.

In chapter 3, we highlight a number of problematic ways in which many contemporary readers—including ourselves, to some extent—have interpreted the Bible, perhaps especially in our own North American context. While our experiences in church and theology have not been identical, some of the traditions that have shaped us fostered a number of assumptions and perspectives that, again, have led us and others to "shackle" Scripture in certain ways. None of our reflections in this chapter are new or unique; we merely hope to summarize in a brief, illustrative way how Scripture needs to be "liberated" from the interpretive shackles that many of us have placed upon it.

The next three chapters then lay out our particular vision for an even more liberative approach to missional hermeneutics. Chapter 4 ("Toward a Vision of the *Missio Dei*") begins to explore the nature and character of God's liberating mission. Chapter 5 ("The Liberating Word") examines the nature and function of Scripture itself. And chapter 6 ("Missional Hermeneutics and Theological Interpretation") considers a range of theological dynamics that intersect with and inform our vision for missional hermeneutics.

The book closes in chapter 7 ("The Practice of Missional Herme-neutics") with an invitation into the posture and process of missional hermeneutics, generally understood, whether or not readers adhere to the specific lines of our constructive proposal. While of course we hope that our readers will find our vision in chapters 4 through 6 to be compelling and worthy of further exploration, reflection, and engagement, chapter 7 is written so as to provide pragmatic guidance for engaging in missional hermeneutics—and in such a way that it should prove useful whether or not readers share all of our perspectives concerning postmodernity. Either way, we believe that missional hermeneutics holds great promise for *liberating Scripture*—in both dimensions of that double entendre! We hope you, our readers, enjoy and benefit from the journey ahead.

PART ONE

Missional Hermeneutics

An Introduction and Invitation

CHAPTER 1

Why *Missional* Interpretation?

IN THIS CHAPTER AND the next, we seek to introduce and invite our readers into a fresh approach to biblical interpretation, known among its theorists and practitioners as *missional hermeneutics*—or, in less technical language, *missional interpretation* (given that "hermeneutics" refers to the practice of and reflection on interpretation). At its most basic level, missional hermeneutics refers to *reading the Bible for participation in the purposes of God*. It is a textured and nuanced approach to biblical interpretation that engages with and draws upon the best of scholarly methodologies and insights, while remaining accessible and deeply useful for ministerial practitioners and laypeople alike.

Some readers—perhaps especially those familiar with the chaotic and often contentious field of biblical scholarship—may question the need for yet another hermeneutic for reading biblical texts. It is true that biblical scholarship is characterized by diverse, complex, and already quite effective interpretive approaches, and newfangled methods seem to come into and out of vogue with regularity. But missional hermeneutics is not merely another flash-in-the-pan attempt to do what has been done well already with other, standard and trusted approaches—including basic, careful, "close readings" of the biblical text.

While biblical scholarship has advanced through the development of a wide variety of astute and often highly technical methodologies, missional hermeneutics is not so much a new methodology as it is a fresh *posture* for scriptural interpretation. In other words, a missional approach to Scripture provides an overarching approach or framework within which the welter of interpretive methodologies can perhaps most fruitfully engage biblical literature such that the Bible's fundamental concerns remain centered and emphasized.

Although this missional perspective is relatively new, it is not a newfangled or innovative method as much as a broad interpretive framework within which we can employ existing and emerging methodologies so as to interpret biblical texts in ways that are consonant with Scripture's purposive and formative dynamics. We will return later to reflect more on what we mean by missional hermeneutics and the role of interpretive methodologies within it, but let us first clarify how the term *missional* has been understood in recent scholarship, since traditional and popular understandings of mission terminology can be quite misleading and problematic. We begin with a brief introduction to some of the wider interpretive context that led to the development of missional hermeneutics.

Anticipating Missional Hermeneutics

In general, mission has not been a major topic of interest in biblical interpretation, scholarly or otherwise. Attention to the Bible and mission came initially from mission practitioners, advocates of missionary outreach, and missiologists, who tended to appeal to certain biblical texts for evidence of early Christian mission (e.g., in the Gospels, Acts of the Apostles, and in some of the Pauline letters) for theological and practical guidance concerning contemporary missionary outreach, and, often as evidence of a Christian mandate to engage in missionary outreach beyond the Christian community and across the globe (see especially Matt 28:16–20). In these contexts, *mission* was typically understood in terms of geographic expansion and evangelistic outreach oriented toward religious conversions. Writers concerned with mission tended to treat the Bible relatively uncritically—without much regard for the methods, insights, or nuances of biblical scholarship, which arguably relegated early exploration of the Bible and mission to something of an internal echo chamber among those who sought to engage the two topics in tandem.

For their part, even today, biblical scholars—already familiar with and influenced by the same *traditional* understandings of mission terminology—typically invoke mission only in specific contexts, namely, when a particular text appears to pertain to evangelistic outreach or geographical expansion beyond the Christian community.[1] Again, because biblical scholars generally presuppose and work with these traditional notions of mission, which regularly equate it with evangelism, outreach, and expansion beyond the community of faith, they tend to use the mission word field (e.g., mission, missionary) narrowly and specifically—namely, whenever mission (traditionally understood) appears to be exegetically relevant in a given scriptural text.

A new and revolutionary theological emphasis on the "mission of God" (in contrast to the traditionally pragmatic emphasis on the church's activity) would begin to take center stage in academic discussions of mission as far back as the Willingen Conference in 1952, but even now, few biblical scholars have approached the biblical canon, whether in whole or in part, from a hermeneutical framework shaped by the *missio Dei*. Obviously, if mission is understood narrowly in terms of human activity—especially evangelism and outreach beyond the community of faith—it can serve as a relevant interpretive framework only for particular portions of the Bible, rather than as an overarching rubric for biblical interpretation. But when mission is understood, first and foremost, in terms of God, something interesting happens. We discover that the Bible itself has a missional character—which is quite different than the traditional assumption that various, discrete examples of mission can be found in particular passages within Scripture. As we will see, missional hermeneutics (which links missiological concerns regarding the *missio Dei* and critical, biblical interpretation) presupposes that the entire canon functions—and can be interpreted—*missionally*.

As a more holistic understanding of mission developed—again, rooted not in ecclesial activity but in the *missio Dei*—some interpreters began to recognize and explore its deeper hermeneutical function and import. Several biblical scholars actively engaged in missiological conversations seeking to illuminate the "biblical foundations for mission"[2] that would ground and underscore the missional identity and activity of the church, with David J. Bosch, preeminent among them.[3] While such work

1. See, e.g., Barram, *Mission and Moral Reflection*.

2. Senior and Stuhlmueller, *Biblical Foundations*.

3. Bosch, *Transforming Mission*. See also, e.g., Blauw, *Missionary Nature*; Hahn, *Mission in the New Testament*; Legrand, *Unity and Plurality*. Also noteworthy in this regard is the Bible Studies and Mission (BISAM) project established in 1976 within the International Association for Mission Studies (IAMS). Carried on mostly by scholars from outside of North America, the project "has been studying the interface between

can be understood as an antecedent of missional hermeneutics, traditional assumptions about mission tended to persist among its practitioners. The New Testament continued to receive disproportionate attention, for example; even biblical interpreters ready to attend to matters of mission found it challenging to "find" mission in the Old Testament. Since mission had been understood traditionally in terms of active evangelistic outreach beyond the community of faith, the Old Testament appeared to be largely devoid of mission, and even the New Testament was understood to contain much that was unrelated to mission. Studies attentive to the "biblical foundations for mission" characteristically emphasized what was perceived to be a "centripetal" form of mission within the Old Testament, whereas mission in the New Testament was understood to be "centrifugal" in nature—and far more ubiquitous. Again, interpreters tended in this work to focus on mission where they found it, but mission had yet to become an overarching interpretive rubric for the entire Bible. While such studies rightly began to place mission at the center of interpretive attention, it would remain for others to press further toward a more thoroughly missional approach to the interpretation of the canon as a whole.

Missional Church and Its Legacy

In recent years, the term *missional* has become a major buzzword in certain Christian circles, especially following the 1998 publication of the groundbreaking volume *Missional Church*,[4] which articulated and expounded on a broad consensus in the field of missiology by arguing that the entire theological project of the North American church needed to be thoroughly recast in *missional* terms.[5] In some ways, our discussion in this book grows out of and extends the work that began in and continues in the wake of *Missional Church*. For the authors of that volume, *mission is to be understood not primarily as an activity* of the church—whether framed in terms of evangelistic outreach, global expansion, numerical growth, or other activities and categories often associated with more traditional understandings of mission, *but rather as a matter of theological and ecclesial identity*, rooted in the nature, character, and holistic purposes

---

the Bible and mission," focusing on the "various ways the Bible is used today in mission" (BISAM, "Aim").

  4. Guder, *Missional Church*. See also Guder, *Called to Witness*, xii.

  5. See Guder, *Called to Witness*, 20–43.

of a sending, trinitarian God. For the church, then, mission is *not* to be understood as one facet of its ministry (namely, engagement beyond the community of faith itself), but, by contrast, as participation within the *missio Dei*, which comprehensively defines, characterizes, and shapes the *entire* identity and *every* activity of the church.

The implications of this seemingly subtle but fundamental shift in perspective—*from* a church *with* a mission *to* a church *defined by* participation in God's mission—are as dramatic as they are extensive. As a shot across the bow of traditional theological reflection and ecclesial identity in North American Christianity, *Missional Church* was a necessary and salutary contribution, and it had a profound effect upon many in both the academy and the church.

Missional Church challenged its readers to conceive of mission more comprehensively—in effect, from the biblical perspective of who God is, what God cares about, and what God is doing. Again, this meant that much of what had been understood traditionally to pertain to Christian mission needed to be rethought. Again, popular and traditional understandings of mission had come to be equated almost entirely with outreach *beyond* the church community—most commonly, in terms of some form of evangelistic or social outreach. While these "missionary" efforts[6] of the church certainly yielded some remarkable results, they have often reflected and perpetuated deeply destructive, dehumanizing theological assumptions and colonizing impulses. *Missional Church* urged readers to embrace a much larger, more holistic notion of mission that would truly reflect the comprehensive mission of the God described in the Bible, one by no means limited to "outreach" among those outside the community of faith. The authors of *Missional Church* chose to employ the adjective *missional*—corresponding to *mission*, understood comprehensively in terms of the *missio Dei*—as a word that could serve as a fresh modifier of nouns (e.g., *missional* theology; *missional* church).[7]

6. The word "missionary" has been used, generally within the traditional, outreach-oriented paradigm, as an adjective (e.g., "missionary" efforts) and as a noun (e.g., that person is a "missionary"). In the *missio Dei* paradigm, reflected, for example, in *Missional Church*, the adjective "missionary" is usually replaced by "missional"; this allows for an adjectival form of the term mission (i.e., "missional"), understood in more holistic, *missio Dei* terms.

7. See Guder, *Called to Witness*, xiii: "The 'al' added to 'mission' was intended to focus attention on the essentially 'missionary nature' of the church, to use the Roman Catholic formulation emphasized by the Second Vatican Council. The constructive intent was connected with a polemic directed against the absence of mission as a major theological

Unfortunately, however, the theological nuancing and ecclesiological implications envisioned by *Missional Church* with respect to *mission* and the adjective *missional* have often been overlooked in subsequent conversations about and contributions to missional thought and practice. Indeed, while *missional church* terminology has become popular in many circles, some of the seminal insights of the *missio Dei* consensus have been engaged with in relatively superficial ways, if not widely forgotten or ignored altogether.

Indeed, since 1998, the word *missional* has appeared regularly, in a wide range of contexts, almost always as an adjective modifying some aspect of church's activity. Unfortunately, for many the term has become little more than a trendy substitute for the more traditional words *mission* and *missionary*, often with little of the biblical and theological depth and breadth that *Missional Church* advocated. Thus, while missional terminology stuck, becoming popular in certain circles almost overnight, a holistic understanding of the *missio Dei* often faded from view as many simply applied missional terminology to traditional and reductionistic understandings of the church's calling and activity.

The popularity and ubiquity of the term *missional* have thus contributed to and resulted in a lack of clarity about its meaning and implications. For example, describing God as a "missionary" can, of course, be done without any disruption of traditional understandings of mission: because we know what traditional, human missionaries do, we can simply imagine God in the same way. In so doing, we run the danger of remaking God in our own image. "Too often mission has been defined by the church's proclivities, rather than by divine purposes. By defining mission as little more than evangelistic outreach, the church ironically assumes that what it does is what God wants it to do."[8] In other words, it is easy to assume that what we do as part of what we have traditionally referred to as "mission" naturally and adequately reflects what God in fact calls God's people to be and do. Allowing the Bible to define what God's purposes are, however—and thus what mission would mean from a divine perspective—makes it more difficult for us to define God on our terms, whether as a "missionary" or otherwise.

---

theme in the centuries of doctrinal work addressing the nature and purposes of the church in Western Christendom."

8. Barram, "Bible, Mission, and Social Location," 47.

Ultimately, the word *missional* conjures up different things in practice, depending on who is using the term and in what contexts. Not surprisingly, missionally oriented language has tended to be used inconsistently and idiosyncratically, with the result that participants sometimes end up speaking past one another even while using the same terminology.[9] For more than two decades, particularly in the context of what has come to be known as the Forum on Missional Hermeneutics,[10] scholars and others have thus been engaged in exploring the hermeneutical issues and implications of the *missio Dei*—and trying to make ever more clear what missional interpretation means and what it involves. As co-chairs of the steering committee for the Forum, we want both to advocate for greater clarity with regard to how God's comprehensive and holistic mission, biblically understood, is best articulated, and to invite further discussion and ongoing exploration—particularly, in this context, with regard to how mission, biblically conceived, intersects with and relates to biblical interpretation.

Sharpening our Terminology: Mission Defined in Terms of Divine Purposiveness

In biblical imagery, God is neither a static principle nor a deity removed from the tumult of human life. Whatever else may be said, the God of the Bible is active and intentional, a God of purpose, creatively and deeply engaged in and with the world. This God is personal, relational, loving, faithful, compassionate, merciful, just—*and* always mysterious and untamed. God's purposeful activity creates, liberates, repairs, reconciles, and re-creates wholeness and shalom in, among, and for human beings—and throughout all of creation.

To the extent that the God revealed in the Bible is purposefully engaged in such activities, fulfilling divine purposes, we can describe God as a God of *mission*. In short, *a purposeful God can be understood as a missional God.* To explain what we mean by way of an overly simplistic analogy, consider

9. Guder, *Called to Witness*, xiii: "Since 1998, the term 'missional' has become a basic concept in global missiological discourse. At the same time, the term took on a life of its own and soon became as much a cliché as a useful theological formulation. It began to appear in a vast range of publications, many of which had no connection with the basic claim, made by the [*Missional Church*] project, that there were major theological issues that needed to be engaged if the church in the West was to be faithful to its calling."

10. For more about the Forum and its work, see chapter 2.

the fact that businesses and organizations have purposes that they seek to enact in the world. When such an entity drafts and codifies a "mission statement," it is communicating its purpose(s) for existing. In order to participate faithfully in and stay true to their articulated *mission*, businesses and organizations must continually ensure that everything they do derives from and remains faithful to their stated purpose(s). Whatever does not grow out of or otherwise further their mission is superfluous and thus subject to recalibration or rejection. Mission, in this sense, keeps businesses and organizations on track and in line with their overarching reasons for existing. Understood in this way, *mission is fundamentally about purpose.* The same is true, we submit, with regard to God and to the church.[11]

It is critical to recognize and acknowledge that God's mission, whatever else we may say about it, does not begin or end with the church. Mission—understood in terms of divine purposiveness—always begins and ends with God. Called and caught up into those purposes, the church does not initiate, define, or control God's mission. While the church has a mission, to be sure, it is always and ultimately a facet of God's larger mission, because the church's purposes, when faithfully grasped and enacted, participate within and further divine purposes. Properly understood, the mission of the church is *always* derivative of divine purposes. This approach has profoundly liberating implications both for how we understand the church's mission and how we participate in it.

Again, mission must be defined in terms of who God is, what God cares about, and what God is up to in creation. Recall again the analogy of the mission statement used by businesses and organizations. Understood in terms of divine purposiveness, mission *defines* the church and everything it does. This is a crucial point with deeply practical implications: mission is *not* limited to activity that happens *outside* of the church among those whom parishioners hope to one day incorporate into their membership. Mission, properly understood, characterizes what occurs *within* the church itself (e.g., worship, pastoral care, education and formation, finance and administration) *no less than what happens beyond it.* Indeed, because mission is first and foremost about God, it is fundamentally a *theological* matter in both nature and effect.[12] This perspective can help to liberate the church to

11. Independently, Wright similarly invokes "mission statement" imagery as an apt analogy (*Great Story and Great Commission*, xii–xiii).

12. Traditional understandings of mission typically relegate it to predominantly practical and logistical concerns, as is illustrated by the fact that seminary courses related to mission continue to be housed within "practical theology" departments, rather than in

be what it is truly called to be and do within the larger purposes of God. It can also help the church acknowledge, repent for, and seek to repair the damage of its colonizing legacy and other widespread, negative effects of its reductionistic understandings of mission, which have all too often functioned to convince millions that Jesus must have had little in common with many of his later followers.[13] Then we can begin to move forward honestly, authentically, effectively, and faithfully with the necessary, painful, and yet ultimately healing work of repair and restoration—which accompanies and must usually precede full reconciliation. God is indeed up to something purposeful—*missional*—both inside and outside the church.

It should be noted that there is an intentionally polemical quality to this description of mission as divine purposiveness. We are consciously and *purposefully* reorienting how mission terminology is understood, and, by implication, how we think about biblical interpretation within that larger framework. Again, the mission of the church has not usually been understood in terms of its participation within the larger mission of God. Rather, as we have already noted, the church has typically defined mission in narrow and ultimately reductionistic ways, focusing especially on Christian *activity* oriented toward the geographic and demographic expansion of the faith. Traditionally, mission—or even more reductionistically and problematically, "missions" (in which the "s" at the end clearly emphasizes activity)—has been understood to involve the extension of Christian belief and affiliation beyond already established, "sending" communities of faith, regularly framed in terms of the salvation of souls and often coupled with colonial expansion. In this traditional paradigm—characteristic of the modern (and predominantly) North Atlantic "missionary" movement—mission

---

departments of "theology" proper. Similar "pragmatic" assumptions concerning mission are often evident in congregations as well.

13. Historically, for example, much of the nineteenth-century missionary movement functioned collaboratively and symbiotically alongside (and often as part of) governmentally sponsored efforts to colonize peoples and territories. Spanish and Portuguese colonial efforts in South America are particular cases in point. British Christians, for their part, tended to assume that their own sociocultural values and patterns, political institutions, economic domination, and moral perspectives went hand in hand with "Christianity"; as a result, they were often quite ready to export those dynamics to those whom they were seeking to evangelize. Some assumed that Africans, upon becoming Christians, would (and should) incorporate an (English-styled) tea time in their daily routines. While overt forms of colonization have become rarer, various subtle forms of colonization continue apace today (e.g., through the maintenance and enhancement of diplomatic, socioeconomic, cultural, racial, and even ecclesial power).

was conceptualized, enacted, and justified in various and often problematic ways, resulting in both tremendously positive outcomes as well as horrifying tragedies and traumas. For many church folk in the West and around the world, traditional understandings of mission are so ingrained as to suggest that they spring from the very core of the Christian faith; for many others, mission is a word that actually merits a "trigger warning," given the harm and pain that it has too often inspired. Either way, the traditional paradigm needed to be replaced with something newer and more faithful to the nature of the *missio Dei*. And, in fact, the legacy of modern mission has necessitated and inspired the rethinking of the term *mission* reflected in both *Missional Church* and in this book as well.

Rethinking Mission

At its core, missional hermeneutics asks the question, how do we go about the task of understanding and interpreting the Bible if the mission of God, or *missio Dei*, is at the center of the enterprise? While mission and theology have been implicitly fused together throughout the history of the church, the explicit advent of *missio Dei* theology as the basis for the life and witness of the church emerged in the ecumenical mission movement of the twentieth century. This impulse was fostered by the International Missionary Council (IMC), which was established in 1921 in the aftermath of the 1910 world missionary conference at Edinburgh. The purpose of the Edinburgh conference was to bring together representatives from mission organizations in order to foster deeper cooperation among them in the task of evangelism. At the time of the conference, "mission" and "evangelism" were generally understood to be synonymous and their practitioners were mostly Western missionaries who participated in the work of Western missionary societies. In this context, Christianity was associated with the West and distinguished from the rest of the world, which was generally understood to be non-Christian. Hence, mission was construed as the evangelistic work of proclaiming the gospel to the non-Christian world outside of the West.

In the decades to come, this perception gradually shifted as the questions raised moved away from pragmatic issues—such as, how can we do evangelistic mission more effectively?—toward more theological questions, such as, what is the basis for mission? It was out of this theological exploration that *missio Dei* theology emerged. The historical impulse was to be found in the work of Karl Barth, who asserted that mission finds its first expression in the life of God rather than in the church. Based on this initial claim, the term *missio Dei* was coined and developed. Essentially, *missio Dei* thinking maintained that the ultimate basis for mission is derived from the life of God rather than the church.

Before the advent of *missio Dei* theology, mission had been understood in a variety of ways: as salvation in which individuals are rescued from the eternal consequences of sinful behavior; as the transformation of cultures in which people from the majority world are introduced to the values and benefits of the Christian West; as church growth, in which Christian congregations expand and survive in times of change; and as social progress in which the world is transformed into the kingdom of God. Those who embraced *missio Dei* theology believed that these various and often competing conceptions of mission needed to be reconceived, and in some cases replaced, so that they would be more faithful to the purposes of God.

From this perspective, mission no longer finds its basis in the activity of the church, but rather in the character and life of God. It is understood as a movement first within the life of God and then from God to the world. In this movement, the church functions as a participant in God's mission and as such, is caught up into God's love for the world. This participation calls forth a response of witness and action consistent with God's missional movement. In the words of German theologian Jürgen Moltmann, "It is not the church that has a mission of salvation to fulfill to the world; it is the mission of the Son and the Spirit through the Father that includes the church, creating a church as it goes on its way."[14] In this same vein, South African missiologist David Bosch asserts, "mission is not primarily an activity of the church, but an attribute of God. God is a missionary God."[15] The ecumenical significance of the basic insight of *missio Dei* theology—that mission finds its ultimate rationale in the life of God—is such that it has been embraced by all the major branches of the Christian church, mainline and evangelical Protestant, Roman Catholic, Eastern Orthodox, and Pentecostal.

14. Moltmann, *Church*, 64.
15. Bosch, *Transforming Mission*, 390.

Challenges Related to Missional Terminology

Given that there are historical and theological challenges (and often, confusion) associated with the word *missional* (as well as with the entire *mission* word field [i.e., mission, missions, missionary, and related terms]), some have understandably questioned whether it might be best to jettison mission terminology altogether, particularly with regard to discussions of biblical interpretation. It has been noted that the specific term *mission* is itself not necessarily a biblical term; in fact, the English word *mission* comes from the Latin *missio*, which itself connotes "sending" (and thus it is not difficult to grasp why traditional understandings of mission have usually been associated with outreach and expansion). Various alternatives have been put forward, including "sending" and "witness," both of which have a rich pedigree. At the same time, those terms are not without problems, either, especially as we search for an interpretive framework applicable for the entire biblical canon.

The imagery of "sending," while biblical, is endemic to certain parts of the Bible, but not to all. *Sending* terminology is particularly characteristic of the Gospel of John (e.g., John 20:21) and it is relevant for much of the prophetic writings and imagery across the canon, but it is not as relevant for the other Gospels or for much of biblical literature. In fact, it is arguable that one of the reasons that it took so long for mission to be taken seriously as a core biblical topic and theme—not to mention, as an interpretative framework—is that it was for so long closely associated with the imagery of sending and being sent (again, as found especially, though not exclusively, in John). As long as mission tended to be understood in terms of sending (as the Latin-based usage in English might imply), it was challenging to find much in the Old Testament that qualified as mission. Again, until relatively recently, mission was understood by missiologists and biblical scholars alike to be a primarily New Testament issue, given that "being sent" and engaging in active, intentional outreach beyond the community is not a widespread concern in the Old Testament. Sending and sent-ness, while of more obvious import in the New Testament, are therefore inadequate as interpretive rubrics for the entirety of the biblical canon.

The same can be said for *witness* terminology. "Witness" is especially relevant in the New Testament books of Luke (e.g., 24:48) and Acts (e.g., 1:8), and, at least in conceptual terms, may arguably be more applicable across the biblical canon than "sending" imagery (since biblical writings could be understood, in effect, as bearing witness to God's nature and activity). At the same time, although "witness" is (like sending) a biblical term, its relevance for the entire canon is not fully clear.

In fact, it is not inappropriate to utilize an essentially non-biblical term such as *mission* to refer to an overarching framework for interpretation. Scholarly interpreters know that it is tremendously difficult to identify any singular biblical word or theme that can definitively capture the sense of the entire Bible. To illustrate, debates about the generating "center" of the canon—such as covenant, incarnation, grace, justification, redemption, reconciliation, and faith—have failed to produce definitive results and widespread agreement. While it may be possible to articulate a thoughtful rationale for each of these terms, none of them captures all that the canon communicates. Indeed, the search for a conceptual or thematic "center" of Scripture may itself be misguided. In any case, when we choose a singular biblical theme or term as our overarching interpretive framework, other themes and terms that do not fit neatly within that framework inevitably receive less attention than they should. The challenges in all of this are real.

Given those challenges, other suggestions for what to call the interpretive perspective that we are seeking to articulate have been made. Among the most promising we have heard are a hermeneutics of "participation," of "vocation," of "healing," or even of "liberation." Despite the strengths that each of these terms may have—including, e.g., an emphasis on human engagement in what God is doing—we believe God's nature and activity are best understood in relationship to human engagement with God through the notion of purpose, both divine and human (expressed in missional terminology).[16] God has purposes, a mission, as do human beings, who are called and caught up into those divine purposes. Indeed, divine purposefulness is what engenders, for example, participation, vocation, healing, and liberation.

16. Note that "vocation"—and even biblical terms such as "apostleship" or "apostolic"—would appear to be viable options for a hermeneutical label focused on contemporary interpretation of biblical texts. The problem is that while these terms to invoke the human side of the divine-human dynamic, they do not seem as applicable to God. While we might perhaps say that God has a vocation, that term seems more appropriately applied to human beings and the church. The same can be said for apostle-related terminology as well. While human apostles have been called into service, it is less clear that apostleship is characteristic of God, at least in terms of how the term is used biblically. These and many other terms, biblical and non-biblical, seem more appropriate in reference to humans than to God (and to the New Testament more than to the Old Testament). By contrast, both God and, by implication, humans, enact purposes—and thus the inherent appropriateness of missional terminology.

Ultimately, we humbly suggest that using *mission* terminology is, in fact, justifiable, even though it is not, strictly speaking, biblical. If the meaning of mission is not narrowly restricted to Latinate "sending" imagery, and we emphasize its common English connotations of purpose and purposiveness, we gain a framework that can be appropriately and equitably applied across the biblical canon without prejudicing any one part of the canon over the other. While "sending" or "witness" may not be especially relevant to every biblical text, we can readily explore the purposive, missional dynamics in *any* text—how divine purposes and purposiveness are being described, how humans are being invited into those purposes, how the text itself functions to form communities for those purposes, and so forth. Enlisting an all-encompassing term like *mission* as a hermeneutical framework may well be a virtue—again, even if it is not biblical—because, understood holistically in terms of purpose, mission is equally applicable to God, to humans, and to all of biblical literature (unlike other options).

Perhaps the most serious and substantive objection to missional terminology is raised by those who find it so tainted and fraught as to be unredeemable, given so much of the historical missionary movement's problematic practice and legacy—associated, as it is, with political and economic colonization, imperial domination, and interpersonal and systemic racism (phenomena which are, of course, interrelated). From this perspective, no amount of updating and clarification can adequately distinguish "mission" (as we are using the term) from the negative things that have been done under the same name. This is a powerful objection—one that we readily acknowledge, understand, and appreciate. Indeed, for just this reason, we have continued to reflect on and engage with the issue of terminology in order to explore potential alternatives to *mission* language. At this point, however, it seems that any alternative terminological choices would probably cause as many problems as they solve.

To be sure, all of this is fraught and difficult. At this stage, we continue to use mission terminology—reconceptualized, as we have discussed, in holistic, purposive terms—although we use the word with humility and flexibility, open to potentially new possibilities that may arise in the future, recognizing that there is significant baggage associated with the term *mission*. We and our colleagues in the missional hermeneutics conversation are not particularly dogmatic about what this emerging form of biblical interpretation should be called; in truth, we are advocating the framework and implications of the approach more than the specific name we use for it.

Until better terminology is developed, though, we believe that "missional interpretation," properly understood, probably remains the best way to describe the approach we are advocating.[17]

Reading a Missional Bible

In order to participate faithfully in God's larger purposes, we need to go back to Scripture as readers to rediscover what God is doing and how God is inviting our participation in that divine mission. In short, we need to read the Bible *missionally*, exploring the ways that it may serve as individual and communal formation for participation in divine purposes. Such an approach to biblical interpretation emphasizes the ways in which biblical texts functioned (for their original readers) and continue to function (for contemporary readers, in every age) as formation for the missional identity and practice of the community of faith in the world.

Exploring Scripture from this kind of missional perspective opens us as readers up to the liberating nature of what the Bible has to say— not as a book of answers or as a collection of rules and doctrines, but rather as an anthology of formative texts, conversations, ponderings, explorations, and questions that can shape our communities so that they are empowered to experience and bear the fruit of God's abundant and life-giving shalom. Perhaps no less significantly, we suggest that reading the Bible from a missional perspective also effectively liberates Scripture from us, its readers, who regularly try to tame, domesticate, and control the Bible—intentionally or otherwise—so that we can be sure that it will communicate to us what we want it to.

By starting with the assumption of a *missio Dei*, in which God is engaged purposively and intentionally in all of creation (as the Bible itself indicates), a missional approach to biblical interpretation attends

---

17. One potential candidate could be the terminology of "calling" (e.g., a hermeneutic of calling), which is not narrowly implicated in the practice and legacy of the missionary movement. It also has the advantage of being oriented to purpose—since God calls humans to participate in divine purposes. Both God and humans are directly linked, biblically and theologically, to "calling." And certainly "calling" terminology has resonance in a wider range of biblical literature than, say, the language of "sending," which makes it more appropriate for use with regard to the entire canon. Even still, "calling" presupposes a purpose or purposes for which the calling occurs. So, because divine purposes logically precede divine "calling" of human beings, there seems to be value in maintaining the priority of "mission" (understood in terms of purpose) over the language of "calling."

especially to who God is, what God cares about, and what God is up to—and, derivatively, how human beings are being called, formed, and equipped to participate in those divine purposes—as the most important considerations for effectively and faithfully interpreting biblical texts. In other words, missional interpretation emphasizes what biblical texts, for their own part, seem most to want to communicate to their readers. The purposes of God (the *missio Dei*) and, again, human participation within those divine purposes, are the ultimate concerns of Scripture and thus the primary and abiding concerns of missional interpretation.

Missional hermeneutics is intentional about allowing and enabling the Bible to say whatever it may want to say. The process is characterized by open-ended curiosity and discovery, exploring what Scripture communicates about the *missio Dei* and thus about the church's role in that mission. Discerning what biblical writers were seeking to communicate in that regard can be clarified in the process of missional interpretation, but the interpretive process need not begin with such conclusions in hand. Likewise, we suggest that missional exploration of Scripture is not beholden to a specific theological system or dictated by particular creedal commitments. This does not mean that missional interpretation proceeds from a vague, wishy-washy, or noncommittal stance. But it does mean that for interpretive purposes, traditional human logics, theological and philosophical systems, and ecclesial loyalties must be held lightly and with deep humility. Scriptural texts are given the freedom to communicate whatever they will—and not merely how and what interpreters may imagine, hope, or anticipate that they will. The adventure begins as we read Scripture from the perspective of that assumption, following biblical texts wherever they lead.

Interpreting Scripture from a Missional Posture

Let us return for a moment to a potential objection that we noted at the outset of this chapter, namely, that readers may justifiably question the need for a specifically missional approach to interpretation. For one thing, a dizzying variety of interpretive methods are already in use today. What is innovative about a missional approach? Again, the short answer is that a missional approach to Scripture is less a new method of interpretation— or even a creative combination of established methods—than it is a fresh posture or framework within which a potentially endless range of interpretive methodologies can be incorporated. Missional hermeneutics provides the presuppositional backdrop for the development and interpretation of biblical texts: the purposes of God and the invitation to participate within that divine mission. Because biblical texts portray a missional God who calls human beings into those purposes, to read Scripture from that vantage point, from a missional posture, is to engage it, as much as possible, within its own internal logics. This is, at the most fundamental level, why missional hermeneutics is both necessary and important.

So, what role do interpretive methodologies play within missional hermeneutics? While missional interpretation does not itself represent a unique interpretive methodology, nor is it characterized by a specific combination of established methods, it readily incorporates and utilizes any and all methods and approaches that may help to illuminate the missional nature and function of biblical texts. While some interpretive methods will undoubtedly prove more salient and fruitful than others, no methodologies need be ruled out from the outset. Missional hermeneutics, again, has more to do with our interpretive assumptions as readers than with the specific methods of inquiry to be used in relation to the biblical text. If, for example, redaction criticism (a scholarly interpretive methodology that has been employed to great effect) helps to highlight something important in the process of comparing biblical texts, as it so often has, then missional hermeneutics chooses to reflect on what redactional insights can contribute when viewed specifically from the perspective of the *missio Dei*. The same is true of other interpretive methods. For missional hermeneutics, there is no reason to avoid or foreclose on any potential means of providing insight into biblical texts because the entire process is centered on thinking about what the Bible most wants to communicate concerning God's mission and human participation in those divine purposes. Missional hermeneutics is thus self-consciously, eagerly, and openly conversant with many methodologies. Anything that can serve to illuminate the *missio Dei* and human participation within it can potentially be useful and salutary.

Interpretive methodologies enable us to examine texts from many different angles, inferring and deducing much from them—historically, socioculturally, literarily, theologically, and otherwise. Still, while traditional and emerging interpretive methodologies have provided myriad insights about biblical texts, there is always a risk that any exegetical methodology will, in effect, speak more loudly than the texts themselves. Conscious of this constant interpretive tension, we invite our readers to consider engaging in missional hermeneutics, which utilizes the best of exegetical methodologies while being oriented specifically toward enabling biblical texts to communicate, as much as possible, about God's purposes and human participation within them.

As we will argue in the second part of this book, a focus on divine purposes, on the divine mission, ends up highlighting the liberative nature of divine engagement in the world, biblically understood, and attending to God's mission functions to liberate the Bible from us as readers—from our misguided tendencies to control, domesticate, and fashion idols out of our biblical and theological presuppositions and commitments. Again, the double-entendre intentionally implied in the title of this book—*Liberating Scripture*—will come clearly into play here. Indeed, it would be fair to say that we begin to experience the Bible's power to liberate us in part *as* we learn to approach it from a missional perspective, since Scripture is then liberated to speak and to form us as it was intended and still seeks to do.

Once again, missional interpretation assumes that the holistic purposes of God—that is, the *missio Dei* (what God cares about and is up to)—along with the invitation to humans to participate in those divine purposes (the mission of the church)—serves as the interpretive key to Scripture. To read the Bible missionally is to recognize that in one way or another biblical texts themselves presuppose, illuminate, and serve to further the larger purposes of God. In effect, we can say that the Bible, in whole and in part, is both a product and a tool of God's mission. Missional hermeneutics assumes that we read Scripture most appropriately when we approach it from this interpretive posture. In the next chapter, we will introduce and briefly explore several specific streams within missional hermeneutics that have developed in relation to established interpretive methodologies within biblical scholarship.

CHAPTER 2

Missional Hermeneutics and Biblical Interpretation

AS WE HAVE ALREADY noted, missional interpretation is centered on the *biblical* assumption that God is active and purposive—in other words, that the biblical God is *missional*. And missional hermeneutics focuses a keen eye on the ways in which, biblically speaking, human beings are called and caught up into those divine purposes. Missional hermeneutics thus explores the biblical text, in whole and in part, in order to discern the formative shape and function of Scripture—specifically, in light of the biblical portrayal of a purposive God and the ways in which the Bible serves to form its readers for participation in divine purposes. These are the fundamental interpretive dynamics that we are exploring in this book. We are, in short, inviting our readers to begin interpreting the Bible from a fresh vantage point, from the perspective of what Scripture reveals about who God is, what God cares about, what God is doing in and throughout the created order—and how human beings are invited and called into participation in divine purposes. Indeed, from the perspective of the *missio Dei*, the Bible's formative shape and function begin to become clearer and more accessible.

So, what does missional interpretation actually look like? And, what does it mean, in practice, to adopt a missional posture for biblical interpretation? As this subfield of biblical hermeneutics enters its third decade, we intend to explore some of the specific areas of focus that have developed within it, which will enable us to see more clearly what missional hermeneutics actually looks like, and what it means, in practice, to adopt a missional posture for interpretation of the Bible. Initially, however, it may first be helpful, at least for readers whose primary frame of reference is not biblical scholarship, to review the classic three-part framework through which interpretation has been understood in biblical research. Doing so will then allow us to situate some of the specific foci of missional hermeneutics within the wider context of biblical interpretation.

The Three "Lenses" of Biblical Interpretation

Biblical interpretation as a whole—and, indeed, the human processes involved in all interpretation, generally—can be characterized in terms of three different but complementary perspectives or lenses. While these three lenses are distinct and developed along different lines in biblical scholarship, they are often employed collaboratively in the actual practice of interpretation. It will be useful to review these three perspectives briefly as we seek to illuminate some of the interpretive "streams" that have developed within missional hermeneutics over the past two decades.

Generally speaking, we can illustrate the process of interpretation—no matter what is being interpreted (e.g., a piece of writing, a movie, a facial expression, or anything else), in fact—in terms of three factors: (1) the thing to be interpreted; (2) the contextual background and historical development of that particular thing; and (3) the interpreter/s who are engaged in trying to make sense of the thing. As a visual metaphor, we might picture a literary *text* to be read; the background and development of that text itself (i.e., whatever lies *behind the text*); and an interpreter who is *in front of the text* reading it.

First, think about the text of this book that you are reading right now. On its pages, you can see words, phrases, and sentences arranged upon the page and combined together in particular ways. In order to interpret this text, you must consider carefully what is actually written on the pages that you are reading, and how that writing is presented. There are a range of important questions to ask. Does the text appear to be prose or poetry? What is its particular genre? How might we describe the writing style and the syntax of the phrases and sentences? All of these things—and much more—can be explored relatively straightforwardly by engaging in what is sometimes described as a "close reading" of the text itself. In this case, the interpretive task is to take stock of—and to seek to make sense of—all of the information (e.g., genre and other literary characteristics such as syntax, setting, style, plot, and so forth) that can be gleaned from *the text itself.* To do this, we pay special attention to what we find on the pages we read. As we will note later, it is crucial in biblical interpretation to recognize and deal appropriately with the great diversity of literary genres contained in the Bible. Inadequate regard for assumptions and expectations relative to ancient genres has regularly led to understandings of Scripture that do not do justice to the literary forms of writing through which its various authors chose to communicate. Moreover, in the case of an anthology of literature—such as the Bible—we may even consider how particular documents and texts that we encounter fit within and relate to the rest of the collection. In biblical literature, this is usually known as canonical criticism.

Second, it is important to recognize that before you can seek to interpret what is written on the pages in this book, a range of interpretively significant things have *already* taken place *behind the text,* as it were, before you've even been able to read it. Authors (and editors)—and the readers that they anticipate engaging with their writings—are all located within particular contexts: historically, geographically, linguistically, philosophically, socioculturally, economically, politically, religiously, and so forth. That is, texts are situated within and reflect a range of contextual frameworks and considerations that relate to what we find in them. Each of those contextual factors can be significant as we seek to interpret the texts we read. Biblical scholars diligently investigate a seemingly endless range of contextual phenomena *behind* biblical texts in order to interpret them in a manner that attends responsibly to the contexts out of which they developed. Doing so requires research that engages a wide swath of historically oriented disciplines and methods.

Moreover, texts do not materialize out of thin air. Everything that we read reflects a prior process of development *behind the text* that may be important for interpreting it. Whatever we find on the written page has been conceived of, written, edited, printed, and published—all before we are able to read it. In biblical scholarship, significant critical attention is paid, for example, to the manuscript history of biblical texts as they are copied and re-copied over time (textual criticism); the likely life situations of ancient communities that are reflected in texts (form criticism); the literary and other sources that are incorporated into texts (source criticism); and the ways that those sources are used and adapted by authors and editors (redaction criticism). In short, both the contextual factors and developmental processes that lay *behind* the things we read are worthy of attention as we interpret texts.

Third, as readers and reading communities, we are "located" contextually when we place ourselves *in front of* texts to read them. Consequently, we cannot but bring our contextually located perspectives into the process of interpreting those texts. That is, none of us comes to the process of interpretation with a "blank slate," as if we could investigate anything apart from our assumptions, preconceptions, previous experiences, biases, and the like. We always engage in interpretation from the contextual "locations" in which we are already socially embedded. As human beings, we cannot do otherwise. So, interpretation does *not* merely involve attention to *the text* under consideration, or what lies *behind* that text (i.e., its historical context and development), but interpretation also inherently involves who we are as readers when we place ourselves *in front of* a text in order to read and seek to make sense of it.

While this third lens was not widely acknowledged or engaged in the initial flowering of biblical scholarship, it is now widely recognized as a critical piece of the interpretive pie. Indeed, biblical scholarship has developed—and continues to develop (often, by adapting from other disciplines)—an often dizzying array of approaches to and methods of textual interpretation that are united in taking seriously the fact that the located nature of readers affects and plays a significant role in making sense of texts. The hallmark of this third lens of biblical exploration is that interpreters self-consciously acknowledge the locations from which they read, intentionally and publicly putting their interpretive cards on the table, so to speak.

Familiar interpretive approaches along these lines include, for example, various forms of feminist and liberationist readings, but, given that all readers are, in fact, "located" (whether or not they acknowledge where they are coming from as readers), this lens serves to highlight the fact that interpretation is never entirely about methodology per se; rather, interpretation is always about the function and significance of posture and perspective. Despite what early biblical scholarship may have assumed, there is no such thing as entirely "disinterested"—that is, completely "objective," bias-free—interpretation. All forms of interpretation are perspectival and contextual, and thus inherently "interested."

To illustrate, while white men have historically tended to dominate biblical scholarship, taking the lead in emphasizing the first two lenses we discussed above, they have not tended to highlight the presence and interpretive function of their own located assumptions and perspectives—at least until relatively recently. By contrast, feminist and liberationist interpreters—as well as readers from many other located perspectives that have been marginalized within traditional scholarship—have been more forthcoming about the "located" lenses through which they read texts. Focusing on the role of readers in interpretation is by no means limited to feminist and liberationist approaches, however. Again, given that all interpretation is located and thus perspectival, the third lens highlights the fact that no matter who is involved in reading a text, we all read texts from "interested" positions and perspectives. No theological reflection can be responsibly understood today as universal or "neutral" theology. It is now widely acknowledged that *all* theological reflection is adjectival in character—located, particular, and limited, whether or not we acknowledge and articulate the relevant adjectives. If we're going to specify that some theology comes from a "feminist" lens, for example, we need to acknowledge that most theologizing has been done from a "male" lens (though this type of theology has rarely identified its particular, located framework and perspectival limitations).

Broadly speaking, biblical scholarship has emphasized each of these three perspectives over the course of its development as a discipline. While each lens can perhaps be discerned in various ways across Christian history and practice before the arrival of modern biblical scholarship, they began to be explored, theorized, and employed far more consciously and intentionally once sustained scholarly inquiry into biblical texts began in earnest, particularly in the mid- to late-nineteenth century. Initially, serious biblical analysis blossomed when researchers began to explore the second of the three interpretive perspectives, namely, the background and development that lay *behind* the biblical texts that we read in our Bibles. In fact, this lens was undoubtedly the predominant focus of biblical scholarship from the nineteenth century until at least the 1970s. An emphasis on the *text itself* came next,[1] followed more recently by research that highlights the reader/s *in front of the text.*

---

1. The emphasis on the final form of the *text itself* developed in response to wider developments in literary studies, as well as because many interpreters found themselves dissatisfied with *behind-the-text* approaches, which, by focusing primarily on historical and developmental factors, sometimes seemed to render the final form of the biblical text something of an afterthought.

Going *Behind* the Text

At least four fundamental assumptions drove (and, to some extent, continue to drive) *behind-the-text* biblical interpretation. First, since biblical authors presumably sought in their writings to communicate with their readers, the meaning of texts must be rooted in what their authors (and/or editors) *intended* to communicate. Second, there must, therefore, be—at least in principle—a single "correct" interpretation of everything in the Bible, corresponding to the *authorial intent* that lay behind it. Third, research into any text (or any portion of a text) must seek out precisely what any given author intended to communicate, and must continue to pursue that intention until it can be (at least theoretically) definitively determined. Early biblical scholarship in this vein often referred naively to "the assured results of scholarship," as if certain mysteries of authorial intention had been solved once and for all. (In recent decades, researchers have tended to be much more circumspect about what can be known definitively.) Fourth, once the authorial intent of any given biblical text is understood, the accuracy of that interpretation should render it universally valid and definitive for any and all readers.

In order to determine authorial intent, it is necessary to gain as much insight as possible into the historical contexts and sociocultural worlds of authors and their audiences. Doing so requires investigation into anything that potentially lay *behind* the texts to be interpreted. As we noted above, exploring what is *behind* texts requires various forms of historical analysis—e.g., text-, form-, source-, and redaction-critical methodologies, which, together, are often traditionally known as "historical criticism."

Recent developments in philosophy and related fields have seriously challenged the assumption that we can ever really get back into the mind of an ancient (and, in fact, any) author enough to discern original intent. Think about works of art—poetry, music, film, visual media, and so forth. In what sense is the meaning of a poem or painting or film defined by what the artist *intended* to communicate? Can an artist control how their work is interpreted or what it "means" after it has been released into the world? Most of us recognize that a work of art can justifiably signify or "mean" something to an interpreter that has nothing to do with what the original artist may have "intended."

Ultimately, authorial intention can continue to serve as a critically valuable interpretive consideration—and, for many scholars, it remains determinative. Certainly, to the extent that we can identify what an author sought to communicate, we should pursue that intention and explore its interpretive implications. Historical-critical scholarship, which, at least implicitly, presupposes some level of authorial intention, provides invaluable insight into biblical texts and the contextual "worlds" *behind* them. In so doing, it offers important interpretive guardrails and parameters within which to assess the historical and contextual plausibility of any textual reading. Still, inspired, in part, by developments in literary research more broadly, biblical scholarship has expanded in recent decades to take into account other issues highlighted by the other two lenses.

Focusing on *the Text Itself*

In the mid- to later-twentieth century, in particular, literary concerns began to gain ascendancy among biblical researchers, especially as the historical-critical search for authorial intent proved to be more elusive than originally anticipated—and, as a consequence, the "assured results of scholarship" were often shown to be far less than assured. Attending to the biblical *text itself*—and, specifically, to the *final form* of the text (rather than upon its historical background or development)—enabled scholars to focus on and emphasize matters such as literary genre, rhetoric, and style; intertextual dynamics; moral and theological content and argumentation; and the interpretive function of texts within the overall shape and content of the biblical canon.

While this "return" to the final form of the biblical text did not necessarily rule out the kinds of historical considerations characteristic of the *behind-the-text* interpretive lens, many scholars did begin to focus almost exclusively on *the text itself.* Many researchers (along with many church folk, it must be said) had grown weary of the ways in which historical-critical concerns often seemed to leave scriptural texts in tatters on the scholarly floor. Sustained work on literary matters—which continues today, largely unabated—refocused attention on the communicative and formative function of texts, both within their original communities and in contemporary contexts.

The goal of this text-centered research is not so much to explore what a given author may have intended to communicate per se, but rather to focus upon and understand the text and its internal dynamics to the extent that they can be discerned on the page. In this context, for example, literary studies of biblical poetry, narrative analyses of the Gospels, and argumentative assessments of biblical letters were published in large numbers. Likewise, canonical criticism emerged, focusing on, among other things, the interpretation of biblical texts in light of the overall shape and character of the biblical collection as a whole. Attention to these literary considerations increasingly brought matters of argumentation and theological import, rather than primarily historical concerns, to the fore.

The key point in all of this is that those engaged in this kind of research do *not* assume that determining authorial intent should be the primary goal of research. Indeed, the "meaning" of a text is not assumed to be restricted—or even primarily oriented—to authorial intent. Rather, meaning is understood in this context to be more open-ended, as texts ultimately operate independently of their original authors and editors. Again, from the perspective of this interpretive lens, texts can be explored quite effectively on their own terms. In fact, scholars in this area assume that we can glean critical insight into biblical texts—including their formative function for reading communities—precisely by attending to their internal (and/or canonical) dynamics.

Ultimately, a turn toward *the text itself* can be understood as something of a corrective move in response to the analytical, historical-critical tendency to disaggregate and dismember the final form of the text. Given that interpretation is about making sense of an object of inquiry—whether, in this case, the Bible, or any other thing to be explored—careful and sustained attention to the object *itself* is undoubtedly necessary.

Readers *in Front of* the Text

Finally, it should be increasingly clear that the third interpretive perspective or lens, which focuses on the role of readers *in front of* the text, involves an assumption that the "located" nature of interpretation is a universal phenomenon, even if that has not always been recognized or acknowledged by scholars engaged in historical-critical ("behind the text") or literary ("the text itself") approaches. As we have noted before, readers and reading communities come to any interpretative activity—including reading biblical texts—from socially contextualized "locations."

At the most basic level, social scientists point to the importance of the contextual "places" from which humans engage whatever we interpret. Because our experiences as human beings occur within a web of social constructs—such as race, gender, and class—we cannot help but be influenced and shaped by those "locations" as we seek to make sense of the world. Of course, there are other contextual factors that also influence what we see and how we interpret; characteristics such as ethnicity, age, bodily ability, religion, geographic context, sexual orientation, educational experience and attainment, and familial culture, among others, also "locate" us as interpreters. In a real sense, given that we see and make sense of the world through our experiences and socially constructed perspectives, we could probably include *any and all* of our experiences and perspectives as locating factors that affect our interpretative activities.

As humans, we reflect complex and ever-evolving amalgamations of our various socially located experiences and perspectives. While each and every aspect of our personal "social locations" may not discernibly shape every interpretive moment, there can be little doubt that, depending on what we are investigating, some of our "locatedness" will indeed come into play. At the most basic level, our personal religious experiences affect how we understand and experience particular forms of worship, theological writings, or rituals and practices. Our economic experiences affect how we think about taxation, the stock market, those without stable housing, and policies concerning health care. Our political experiences—from participation in the democratic process to our media consumption—shape how we think about the political dynamics at play in our communities and the wider society. The effects of social location are both far reaching and unavoidable.

Again, no one enters into a process of interpretation from a "neutral" location. We are all shaped and formed by our experiences of the world, and thus we are naturally and inevitably "biased." We cannot avoid bias by ignoring it, and our biases affect our experience of the world despite any attempt to deny that we have and are shaped by them. Of course, we must avoid allowing our biases to harden into prejudices. That happens when we are unwilling to allow new experiences to reshape and reform our biases and the interpretive tendencies that go with them.

Not surprisingly, our social locations, understood in the broad sense that we are suggesting here, need not—indeed, should not—remain static. The social contexts within which race, gender, social class, and our other "locations" are understood change and develop over time. We continue to have new experiences as we live our lives, and so we are not exactly the same people today that we were last year, last week, or even last night. Indeed, as our range of experiences grows, our perspectives and biases can and, to some extent, will change. As we will see later, this is a critically important consideration for those of us in the church.

Focusing on the role of readers in interpretation highlights the necessity of understanding that textual meaning is a highly complex matter. Texts do not simply possess intrinsic meanings entirely independent of the contexts within which they are interpreted. Meaning is, at least in part, contingent upon the locations within and from which texts are being engaged. Textual meaning will always be to some extent multivalent, as different readers and reading communities see and hear different things from the perspective of their various social contexts.

It is important to recognize that located readings of texts are no more "biased" than interpretation done from either of the other two lenses. Again, all interpretations reflect located biases; no interpreter is immune from this dynamic. Researchers who focus on readers and their communities intentionally make (at least part of) their locatedness explicit as part of the interpretive process. By contrast, practitioners of historical-critical and literary approaches, who focus primarily on the background and development of the text or on the text itself, tend to be relatively less directly forthcoming about their interpretive locations. Whether or not we make our biases public, they inform what we choose to explore, the questions we ask, and how we make sense of what we find. Unarticulated biases are not neutral; they still affect our interpretation.

Again, *in front of the text* interpretative approaches recognize and highlight the fact that our social locations affect what we see in texts, as well as how we react to and make sense of them. Indeed, our reactions to texts are often effective pointers toward our locatedness. Privileged North American readers, for example, often perceive Jesus's conversation with the rich man in Mark 10:17–31 as bearing an inherently negative message—one that has more to do with danger and a warning than good news. To be sure, Jesus encourages the man who, perhaps ironically, is missing "one thing," to "go, sell what you own, and give the money to the poor, and you will have treasure in heaven; then come, follow me" (v. 21).[2] Because the wealthy man was unwilling to do that, he "went away grieving." Those who read this story from a location of wealth and privilege might find themselves concerned about what they would potentially lose if they were to follow the advice that Jesus gave to the man. Jesus then further drives home the challenge of wealth (and presumably the sense of security, privileges, and worldview that

2. Unless noted otherwise, all scriptural quotations are from the NRSV.

34

come with it): "It is easier for a camel to go through the eye of a needle than for someone who is rich to enter the kingdom of God" (v. 25). This does not sound like especially good news for wealthy people, even though Jesus goes on to affirm that "for God all things are possible" (v. 27).

And yet, at the same time, it is worth noting that the story may well be *full* of good news for readers who approach it from less privileged socioeconomic locations. Note that Jesus advises the man to give the proceeds from the sale of his possessions *to the poor* (v. 21). The wealth redistribution that would result from this man choosing to follow Jesus would be entirely good news for those with much more limited resources.[3]

Different locations often lead to different interpretations. No one reader—or community of readers—sees the whole picture. Our located lenses may help us see some things clearly, while blinding us to others. This is true for all of us, and so we undoubtedly need each other. Diversity is thus a strength and gift in this regard.

Ultimately, we could say that *in front of the text* approaches are less about specific interpretive methods than they are about the interpretive places from which and the postures with which we come to the process of textual investigation. In many cases, in fact, scholars who utilize *in-front-of-the-text* approaches combine an emphasis on the located nature of interpretation with historical and literary methods characteristic of the first two interpretive lenses, so that two or even three of the perspectives are intentionally placed in dialogue all at once. Indeed, each of the three lenses can be utilized in combination with any or all of the others, though the first two have tended to be used in isolation more often than the third has been. With this initial introduction to the three classic lenses of interpretation in hand, we are now prepared to review the historical development of missional hermeneutics. Next, we will explore how missional hermeneutics fits within the larger arena of biblical scholarship.

The Development of Missional Hermeneutics

Informed and shaped by the *missio Dei* perspective, the Gospel and Our Culture Network (GOCN) played a significant role in the early exploration and development of missional hermeneutics. Inspired by conversations in Great Britain during the 1980s that had arisen in response to Bishop

---

3. For a fuller discussion of this text along these lines, see Barram, *Missional Economics*, 154–70.

Lesslie Newbigin's work, the GOCN devoted itself to exploration of the intersection between culture and the Christian gospel, seeking to foster fresh missional reflection and congregational engagement within a North American context that during the twentieth century had become more of a mission field than a missionary launchpad. Indeed, it was research by the GOCN that led to the groundbreaking volume, *Missional Church*, written by leading theological voices within the Network. Among its game-changing contributions, that book anticipated the need to explore how a theological framework defined and characterized by the *missio Dei* would reorient and reshape biblical interpretation.

In 1998, the same year that *Missional Church* appeared, James V. Brownson published *Speaking the Truth in Love: New Testament Resources for a Missional Hermeneutic*. A New Testament scholar and member of the GOCN Board—and apparently the first to coin the term *missional hermeneutic*[4]—Brownson clearly and insightfully examined the gospel and culture dynamics at the heart of the New Testament, leading directly to the conversation that would soon develop into the subdiscipline of missional hermeneutics.

Indeed, interest in mission as an interpretive framework surged following the publication of *Missional Church* and *Speaking the Truth in Love*. The decisive turning point that would initiate the development of missional hermeneutics came in 2002, when, at the inspiration of theological ethicist Jeff Greenman, Tyndale Seminary (Toronto) sponsored a breakfast gathering featuring Brownson as the keynote speaker, during the Annual Meetings of the American Academy of Religion (AAR) and Society of Biblical Literature (SBL). Brownson's presentation, entitled "An Adequate Missional Hermeneutic," effectively inaugurated the focused and sustained scholarly work on missional hermeneutics that continues to this day.

Over the next two years, Tyndale Seminary would sponsor two more breakfast keynotes during the Annual Meetings of the AAR/SBL, each given by a biblical scholar (Michael Barram, 2003; Grant LeMarquand, 2004). Attendance at these initial gatherings was sufficient to suggest that further discussion was warranted. A small group of individuals affiliated with the GOCN began to organize a conference session to be held in 2005. That gathering would feature three papers, by Christopher J. H. Wright, Colin Yuckman, and James C. Miller. As a means of fostering the emerging dialogue, the previous keynote presenters—Brownson, Barram, and

4. Hunsberger, "Mapping."

LaMarquand—each served as a respondent for one of the papers. It became clear to the 2005 organizers that an important conversation was developing, and that future conference gatherings were in order.

Beginning in 2006, the GOCN began to sponsor sessions held during the annual AAR/SBL conferences. The 2006 session featured two papers, one by missiologist Michael Goheen, and the other by Barram. Representing something of a fork in the road in the emerging conversation, the two presentations exemplified divergent trends in focus and methodology that would, in certain ways, come to characterize the development of missional interpretation. While Goheen's paper ("Notes Toward a Framework for a Missional Hermeneutic") foreshadowed what has become a consistent emphasis in his work on the grand story of God's mission across Scripture, Barram ("'Located Questions' for a Missional Hermeneutic") signaled a postmodern and methodologically inductive turn toward the function and formation of reading communities socially located within the larger missional purposes of God. The juxtaposition of the papers, although unplanned by the organizers, was both striking and generative. The kind of canonically focused, narrative orientation in missional interpretation modeled by Goheen was gaining attention, informed and inspired especially by influential voices such as Wright. At the same time, Barram's emphasis on the kinds of "missional questions" that missionally located reading communities need to ask of Scripture (and be asked by it) signaled that other serious interpretive dynamics would also merit attention going forward.

In 2007, exegetical and pedagogical concerns took center stage, as missiologist Darrell Guder and biblical scholar Ross Wagner presented on their experiences co-teaching a Princeton Theological Seminary course on reading Philippians missionally.

The 2008 sessions were particularly significant: George R. Hunsberger, a missiologist and founding general coordinator of the GOCN, gave what has probably become the single most influential paper presented in the Forum's history: "Proposals for a Missional Hermeneutic: Mapping a Conversation." Hunsberger carefully categorized and assessed the prior work on missional hermeneutics up to that point. His insightful and nuanced contribution provided a clear and useful framework for understanding not only the various interpretive tendencies that had arisen by 2008 but also the differences between them. Hunsberger's analysis represented a watershed moment in the development of missional hermeneutics as it provided the requisite framing and interpretive nomenclature for the emerging subfield, and it continues to provide guidance for ongoing scholarship.

In 2009, the steering committee adopted the name "The GOCN Forum on Missional Hermeneutics" for its ongoing work. Since that year (other than one brief three-year period), the Forum has been recognized as an Affiliate Program of the Society of Biblical Literature. After several years (2005–2010) in which a single conference session was held annually, the Forum began to sponsor multiple sessions each year (two each from 2011 to 2013, and three each year beginning in 2014). In 2019, the steering committee of the Forum, which had been chaired by Barram since 2005, became independent from the GOCN, and the steering committee of the Forum on Missional Hermeneutics began to pursue status as a non-profit organization. Barram was joined by John Franke as co-chair of the steering committee, and the productivity of the Forum on Missional Hermeneutics has continued to increase over the years, both in terms of sponsorship of conference events and wider publication.

Developmental Stages

In retrospect, three fairly clear stages in the development of the Forum on Missional Hermeneutics can be identified. For the first several years (2002–2008), conference sessions were focused organically on initial theorizing about what a missional hermeneutic might entail. Then, in a second stage, from about 2009 through 2015, sessions focused on the exploration of various texts and themes. In the process, the streams of missional emphasis highlighted by Hunsberger were put into practice—sometimes consciously, and at other times less intentionally—enabling them to be tested and clarified. In this stage of its development, the Forum intentionally sought out and benefited from the participation of several scholars who had not been directly involved in the work of missional hermeneutics (Stephen F. Fowl [2009]; Suzanne Watts Henderson [2010]; Klyne Snodgrass [2011]; Richard B. Hays [2013]; Mark Labberton [2015]; and Benjamin T. Conner [2015]), each of whom served as an invited respondent to papers during a particular conference session. Thus, while those closely associated with the Forum often participated in conference sessions (e.g., as presenters, presiders, and respondents), the development and assessment of missional hermeneutics was not carried out in isolation. Other guests, in book review conversations with Forum panelists, reflected on missional dynamics—or, in some cases, missionally adjacent themes—within their own work. In 2011, the Forum reviewed Michael J. Gorman's *Reading Revelation Responsibly: Uncivil Worship and Witness: Following the Lamb into the New Creation* (Eugene: Cascade, 2011); C. Kavin Rowe's *World Upside Down: Reading Acts in the Graeco-Roman Age* (New York: Oxford University Press, 2009) was discussed in 2012; renowned New Testament scholar N. T. Wright joined a Forum panel for a conversation in 2014; and Gorman's *Becoming the Gospel: Paul, Participation, and Mission* (Grand Rapids: Eerdmans, 2015) was reviewed in 2015.

A third discernible stage in the development of missional hermeneutics began in approximately 2016, when the emphasis of Forum sessions shifted to focus on the interpretive dynamics pertaining to contemporary, "located" reading communities. Since Barram's 2006 presentation, this concern for readerly dynamics in missional interpretation had continued to receive attention, though it tended to be overshadowed by both historical-contextual concerns and interest in canonical-narrative dynamics. In 2016, however, intentional and sustained emphasis began to be placed on reading communities and their formation. Topics during this period included migration (2016); politics and citizenship (2017; 2018); the legacy of James Cone (2019); contextual interpretation of the Hebrew Scriptures (2019); the interpretive positionalities of women (2020); reparations (2020); historical and contemporary problematics pertaining to the terminology and grammar of missional hermeneutics (2020); and whiteness (2021).

In addition, book review sessions continued to be a regular feature of Forum gatherings: James Brownson's *Speaking the Truth in Love*, in a nearly twenty-year retrospective, was reviewed by an invited panel in 2016; Henning Wrogemann's *Intercultural Hermeneutics, Vol. 1* (Grand Rapids: IVP Academic, 2016) received similar attention in 2018; Barram's *Missional Economics: Biblical Justice and Christian Formation* (Grand Rapids: Eerdmans, 2018) was reviewed in 2019; and a panel explored Franke's *Missional Theology: An Introduction* (Grand Rapids: Baker Academic, 2020) in 2021.

Most recently, sessions in 2022 included a participatory workshop on missional hermeneutics led by Michael Barram, and a conversation with Pauline scholars Michael J. Gorman and Lisa Bowens (moderated by Franke) on the influence and impact of missional hermeneutics in their own work.

Enthusiasm for and commitment to the ongoing project of missional hermeneutics continues to grow among members of the steering committee of the Forum and those attending the sessions it has been sponsoring. The future of missional hermeneutics as an emerging subfield of biblical interpretation appears promising, and it will be interesting for those aware of and engaged in this innovative interpretive approach to follow its ongoing conversations, research, and publication projects—and to consider its potential influence and formative significance within the church and that academy, both in the near future and in the longer term.

Situating Missional Hermeneutics within Biblical Scholarship

As noted above, George Hunsberger presented a 2008 paper that highlighted four discernible "streams" of emphasis in early missional interpretation. This initial attempt to "map" some of the primary interpretive tendencies within the movement was eventually published—first, in 2011, and then in an updated form in 2016—and it quickly became the most widely recognized point of reference for understanding and describing missional hermeneutics.[5] Hunsberger's work succinctly demonstrated that those who were developing early proposals for missional interpretation were already approaching the task with diverse assumptions, perspectives, methodological tendencies, and areas of focus. The four "streams" identified by Hunsberger offered an early, helpful taxonomy for categorizing and distinguishing between the varied interests and emphases that had begun to emerge. Eventually, a fifth stream was adopted by the Forum on Missional Hermeneutics, and, on occasion, suggestions for other potential streams have been made.

While the four streams initially described by Hunsberger partially reflect the three classic lenses of interpretation that we have highlighted in this chapter, the number and expansive nature of the stream metaphor—again, five, with the potential that others might still be added—could lead to confusion about how missional hermeneutics relates to and furthers biblical interpretation, and may even obscure what is at stake in articulating the need for a missionally oriented approach to interpretation within the larger world of biblical scholarship. Thus, while acknowledging the Forum's continuing indebtedness to Hunsberger's work in what follows in the rest of this chapter, we intend to shift the imagery in our brief analysis so as to attempt to situate the various "streams" of missional

---

5. See Hunsberger, "Proposals"; Hunsberger, "Mapping." All citations are from the latter (2016) version.

hermeneutics within the three traditional interpretive lenses that we have already discussed. This should both clarify what is involved in missional hermeneutics and enable our readers to grasp more readily and fully how it fits within and furthers biblical scholarship.[6]

As we begin, it bears repeating again that missional hermeneutics is not so much an interpretive methodology as an interpretive posture or approach. It is not methodologically restrictive; similar to many interpretive approaches (e.g., feminist, liberationist) that incorporate a range of exegetical methodologies, missional hermeneutics is open to any and all methods that may shed light on the ways that the Bible reveals and articulates the divine mission and forms human beings for participation in it.

Reading the Bible *Missionally*

The most widely recognized and influential "stream" within missional hermeneutics maps directly onto the second of the interpretative lenses we discussed above, which is focused on the final form of *the text itself.* The Bible suggests repeatedly, in various ways and literary contexts, that God is at work in bringing about divine purposes—and actively invites God's people to participate in them. Indeed, the literary character and canonical nature of the Bible suggests the contours of—and some clear specifics pertaining to—an overarching "story" of divine mission. Rooted especially in the work of biblical scholar Christopher J. H. Wright, with noteworthy contributions from missiologist Michael W. Goheen[7] and others, this particular lens reflects a presuppositional and orienting framework within missional hermeneutics.

In *The Mission of God: Unlocking the Bible's Grand Narrative*, Wright argues that to read the Bible appropriately is to read it missionally, attending to the canonically shaped, overarching story of God's purposive mission and the divine invitation to participate as God's people in those larger purposes. While recognizing the manifest diversity across the Bible, Wright understands God's mission—which he views more in terms of divine purposes than in narrowly traditional evangelistic or "sending" terms—as linking the collection of biblical literature together in a kind of "grand narrative":

6. For a slightly different, but overlapping analysis of the development of missional hermeneutics and the "streams" within it, see also Barram, "Missional Hermeneutics."

7. See Goheen, *Light to the Nations.*

> The Bible renders to us the story of God's mission through God's people in their engagement with God's world for the sake of the whole mission of God's creation. The Bible is the drama of this God of purpose engaged in the mission of achieving that purpose universally, embracing past, present and future, Israel and the nations.[8]

Along with Wright, those who emphasize the narrative shape of mission in the Bible attend to the full range of literary matters pertinent to textual interpretation (e.g., genre, style, narrative characteristics, argumentation, intertextuality), including canonical criticism. As the interpretive lens concerned with the final form of *the text itself* emphasizes, there are multiple literary and argumentative contexts at play in relation to any given biblical text. At the risk of oversimplification, any particular scriptural passage is located contextually (1) within the material that immediately surrounds it; (2) within the larger biblical document in which it appears; and (3) within the overall shape of the canon.

From the perspective of this text-centric lens, missional interpretation essentially involves a twofold task: to discern the "story" of God's mission across Scripture (including human participation in that missional story) and to examine individual passages in light of and in relationship to that overarching mission. These emphases are both interdependent and cyclical. Interpretation moves from and between the broad narrative framework and particular texts, as each emphasis informs and deepens the insights and understandings of the other. While a general storyline, from creation to new creation, may appear to emerge relatively straightforwardly, definitive delineation of God's missional purposes may be less so, however. The diversity of specific passages across the canon, many of which do not fit neatly into an overall narrative pattern, inform and nuance the interpretive framework provided by the larger story. Likewise, the meaning and import of particular passages is often clarified as they are considered within the larger story of the divine mission across the canon.

One of the primary contributions of missional hermeneutics—and perhaps of this stream, in particular—is that mission is revealed and understood to be a valid and necessary interpretive rubric for all of Scripture.[9] Mission is not merely evident in certain passages (e.g., the so-called "Great

---

8. Wright, *Mission of God*, 22; see also Wright's short and highly accessible recent volume, *Great Story and Great Commission*.

9. See, e.g., Barram, *Mission and Moral Reflection*.

Commission" in Matt 28:16–20) that appear to emphasize evangelistic outreach (i.e., "mission," traditionally understood).[10] Rather, mission—understood in purposive terms—becomes a hermeneutical lens through which to examine *every* biblical text, whether or not a given passage has ever been understood to pertain in any way to traditional understandings of mission. From this perspective, the Bible does not merely contain evidence of mission (as traditional understandings of mission imply), but as readers we find ourselves exploring *a missional Bible*.

The point is not that a missional hermeneutic is relevant only when discrete biblical texts seem to envision evangelism or other forms of outreach, but rather that every text, canonically framed, participates in some way within a larger story of God's purposiveness. So, whether or not particular documents or textual pericopes have anything to do with outreach, this first "stream" presumes and affirms that they participate somehow within the *missio Dei* as narrated broadly across Scripture—and that, from that vantage point, they can be approached, hermeneutically, from a missional perspective.

Widespread attention to the missional story across Scripture is undoubtedly indicative of the influence of Wright's scholarship, in particular, as the work he and others have contributed has emphasized quite effectively the need for and priority of missional interpretation. Those familiar with the general notion of "missional interpretation"—but perhaps largely unfamiliar with ongoing scholarly discussions and debates about it—may *incorrectly* assume, however, that approaching the Bible with a missionally oriented narrative lens *is*, in itself, what it means to engage in missional hermeneutics.[11] In fact, this narrative approach is but one among a number of missionally focused interpretive perspectives.[12] At the same time, although it is inaccurate and misguided to restrict missional hermeneutics to this text-centric perspective, there is widespread agreement within this emerging subfield that a discernible emphasis on an overarching *story* of God's mission across the canon is important for appropriate interpretation of the biblical text, and the various streams within missional hermeneutics

10. Wright offers a helpful and more holistic corrective to the traditional interpretation of Matt 28:16–20 in *Great Story and Great Commission*.

11. Such an assumption may be reinforced when publications treating "missional interpretation" focus overwhelmingly, if not exclusively, on "text-centric," "story-oriented" readings of biblical texts. For an example, see Goheen, *Reading the Bible Missionally*.

12. As Wright himself points out in *Great Story and Great Commission*, 1–11, 38, 141.

generally presuppose this narrative approach to the biblical text even as they emphasize other facets of interpretation.[13]

The Missional Function of the Bible

Unlike the first missional hermeneutics stream identified by Hunsberger, the second is not as easily mapped onto a single interpretive lens. Instead, the second stream, associated originally with the work of missiologist Darrell Guder, is probably best understood as a combination of both *text itself* and *behind the text* concerns. On the one hand, this second stream focuses closely on the contents and argumentative dynamics of biblical texts themselves, especially attending to the ways in which they seem to equip communities of faith for participation in God's mission in the world. So, in that sense, *the text itself* continues as a primary concern here. At the same time, the second stream attends to the historical and social contexts within which biblical documents seem to have arisen, reflecting the kinds of historical-critical concerns associated with a *behind-the-text* lens. Guder—and others whose work engages this second stream—presumes that there is, *behind* biblical texts, a certain authorial (and presumably, a divine) intentionality. Biblical documents do not simply equip and shape communities of their own accord; there are, in fact, writers and audiences in particular contexts whose concerns and situations are reflected in them. Thus, we can explore the formative function of scriptural texts by seeking as much contextual information *behind* them as possible. For example: what kinds of formation did the authors and editors of biblical documents intend to effect through their writings? What contextual situations did they—and their intended, original audiences—find themselves in that led to what we find in the texts? These are exactly the kinds of historical-critical questions that traditional, *behind-the-text* scholarship seeks to explore.

It is not a literary accident that biblical texts appear to equip communities for participation in the divine mission. Indeed, biblical documents seem to manifest a purposive function regardless of how they have been received by faith communities down through the centuries. That is, the missional character and function of biblical texts is not dependent on whether any particular community of faith recognizes those dynamics within the documents it reads. The second stream presumes that the apparently purposefully equipping function of biblical writings is rooted in a

13. See, e.g., Hunsberger, "Mapping," 52.

missional intentionality reflective of both the biblical authors and the God into whose mission they and their readers have been invited and called to participate. Both the equipping intent and formative effect of biblical texts are of critical importance for adequate interpretation. As Hunsberger explains this stream, "the *aim* of [missional] biblical interpretation is to fulfill the equipping purpose of the biblical writings,"[14] essentially by illuminating and drawing out the implications of the missional formation already discernible in the texts.

It should be noted that Guder is explicit about his concern for the ongoing missional formation of communities of faith;[15] that much is true, in fact, of every missional interpreter whose work engages this second stream. Still, the primary exegetical and interpretive emphases here are placed on discerning how ancient authors and editors purposefully formed their addressees for their individual and communal roles within the divine mission through what they wrote. The assumption is that as we discover the historically contextualized processes and effects of missional formation among the early Christian communities evident in and in relation to biblical texts, we can then seek to apply those discoveries to contemporary communities in subsequent generations. This interpretive move echoes a common distinction often made in traditional, historical-critical scholarship between what a text *meant* (in its original context) and what it *means* (in subsequent, contemporary contexts). While Guder and his "stream two" colleagues do not maintain this distinction as strictly as traditional *behind-the-text* approaches typically have, there is still implicit in this stream something of a tendency to move from exegetical result to contemporary application (as is standard in historical-critical studies).[16] Our next stream seeks from the outset to bridge that "application gap" by taking stock of the interpretive role of contemporary readers and reading communities in every generation from the outset.

14. Hunsberger, "Mapping," 53.

15. See Guder's suggested questions for missional Bible study, which amply demonstrate this contemporary concern: "How does this text evangelize us?"—which Guder calls "the gospel question." "How does the text convert us (the change question)? How does the text read us (the context question)? How does the text focus us (the future question)?" And finally, "How does the text send us?"—which Guder calls "the mission question" ("Unlikely Ambassadors," 5). As Guder notes, some of these questions may be more relevant in certain cases than others.

16. In theory, at least, practitioners of this second stream recognize that interpretation proceeds in a kind of hermeneutical spiral that iteratively bends in circular fashion from one to the other and back again.

Reading the Bible from a Participatory Location within the Mission of God

The third stream within missional hermeneutics, emphasized especially in Michael Barram's work, is key to the approach to missional interpretation proposed in the second half of this book. This stream moves the primary point of reference from both the biblical *text itself* (stream one) and the contextual phenomena *behind it* (stream two) toward the readers of the Bible who find themselves *in front of the text*. As Hunsberger puts it, this stream "shifts the perspective by looking at the character of a missional hermeneutic from the other side of the coin: from the position of the community being thus formed."[17]

As we have already noted, a full accounting of textual interpretation requires attention to the ways in which readers *in front of* texts participate in the interpretive process and thus contribute to their meanings. Drawing on postmodern insights in this regard, many recent interpretative approaches within biblical scholarship have emphasized the role of readerly perspectives—and, in particular, the interpretive significance of social location. As we have repeatedly affirmed, where readers are "located" historically and socioculturally matters. Readerly location influences what we notice, what we recognize, and thus what we see and hear. And the reverse is also true: our interpretive locations can influence what we fail to notice, what we fail to recognize, and thus what we fail to see and hear.

Since the Christian community is called and caught up into the larger purposes of God, the *missio Dei*, *it finds itself in a social location characterized by participation in the divine mission.* Readers, embedded as they are in tangible, real-life human contexts, begin to notice, recognize, and see and hear new things in the biblical text, as well as new implications arising from it. As they approach the Bible with their embodied and embedded questions and concerns, readers start to recognize that their participation within God's missional purposes locates them within a larger, divine framework, vision, and movement. And thus they begin to see and hear the Bible in terms of that *missio Dei*, and to read and encounter Scripture *missionally*, from the vantage point of their social location *within* that divine mission. And when readers approach the Bible from such a "missional location," Scripture itself becomes liberated to speak on its own—missional—terms.

17. Hunsberger, "Mapping," 56.

A liberative dynamic unfolds as readers *in front of the text* are taken seriously in the interpretive process. In general, liberative hermeneutics is self-consciously inductive and contextual, bringing to the biblical text concrete, on-the-ground concerns and questions, and returning to the located context from the text in a praxis-oriented cycle. For example, poor, vulnerable, and otherwise marginalized readers often see things in the biblical text—or perhaps recognize some of the implications of the text—that wealthier and otherwise more privileged readers miss. The text seems to speak anew. New interpretive possibilities emerge. And voices previously unheard find space, utilize agency, and begin to share the interpretive power previously afforded primarily to others. Again, a liberative dynamic unfolds as the Christian community begins to recognize how the Bible reflects, testifies to, and fosters the larger mission of God—and diverse human participation within it.

Of course, Christian communities are found in myriad different locations. Participation in the purposes of God is to be embodied locally and concretely. It is not to be reduced to an idealized theological metaphor; rather, the church's missional participation must be lived out within the dynamics of time and space. Real humans are always socially located with and among other real humans. Framing missional hermeneutics in this way engages the postmodern recognition concerning the locality—and thus the intrinsic diversity—inherent in all interpretation: while diverse communities are invited to participate in the same divine purposes and thus all communities share a fundamentally "missional locatedness" within the *missio Dei*, the specific character of each communal location obviously differs. Inasmuch as no two communities share an identical missional location, the specific shape of their participation within the *missio Dei* may look different in those embodied contexts.

Given such manifest diversity among missional locations, how do Christians in different situations read and interpret Scripture faithfully and appropriately? As Barram has argued elsewhere, missionally "located" questions become imperative:

> Ultimately, a viable missional hermeneutic will not be characterized by a set of unique exegetical methods, nor will broad sketches of the *missio Dei* as revealed in Scripture end up being its primary contribution. Rather, a missional hermeneutic will self-consciously, intentionally, and persistently bring to the biblical text a range of focused, critical, and "located" questions regarding the church's purpose in order to discern the faith community's calling and task

within the *missio Dei*. Such questions will be inherently contextual—rooted in the fundamental conviction that we read the biblical text as those who have been drawn into the larger purposes of God. Ultimately, to read the Bible from a missional perspective is not an eisegetical enterprise but merely an honest acknowledgment of our primary interpretive location as we seek to read the Bible more faithfully today. In that sense, the "social location" of the people of God is at the very heart of a missional hermeneutic.[18]

Here are a few examples of such questions that may have special resonance for North American Christian communities of faith:[19]

- How does our reading of a given text demonstrate humility —recognizing that we see and understand only in part?

- Does our reading of the text challenge or baptize our assumptions and blind spots?

- In what ways are we tempted to "spiritualize" the concrete implications of the gospel as articulated in this text?

- How does the text help to clarify appropriate Christian behavior —not only in terms of conduct but also in terms of intentionality and motive?

- Does our reading emphasize the triumph of Christ's resurrection to the exclusion of the kenotic, cruciform character of his ministry?

- In what ways does this text proclaim good news to the poor and release to the captives, and how might our own social locations make it difficult to hear that news as good?

- Does our reading of the text reflect a tendency to bifurcate evangelism and justice?

- Does our reading of this text acknowledge and confess our complicity and culpability in personal as well as structural sin?

- In what ways does the text challenge us to rethink our often-cozy relationships with power and privilege?

18. Barram, "Bible, Mission, and Social Location," 58.

19. Originally published in Barram, *Missional Economics*, 36–37. Further questions to guide missional interpretation of texts are provided in chapter 7.

- How does this text expose and challenge our societal and economic tendencies to assign human beings and the rest of creation merely functional, as opposed to inherent, value?

- Does the text help clarify the call of gospel discipleship in a world of conspicuous consumption, devastating famine, rampant disease, incessant war, and vast economic inequities?

- How does the text clarify what love of God and neighbor looks like in a particular context?

- How does this text clarify what God is doing in our world, in our nation, in our cities, and in our neighborhoods—and how may we be called to be involved in those purposes?

- Does our reading allow the text the opportunity to define everything about our mission in the world—including our assumptions, processes, terminology—everything?

To be sure, "the important point is not that every question is equally applicable to every community, but simply that missionally 'located' questions have inherently 'located' implications for the communities who ask them."[20] Faith communities must continue to ask critical, missional questions about who God is, what God cares about, and what God is up to—and how God (through the Bible and the presence and guidance of the Spirit) intends to continue to form them for their ongoing participation within the *missio Dei*. Further, they must themselves be ready to be questioned by God (through the Bible and the presence and guidance of the Spirit) with regard to their participation in the *missio Dei*. In every case, these questions will be missionally located—with implications to be embodied locally and concretely.

Additional Streams

The three streams identified by Hunsberger that we have discussed have been the primary focus of scholarly attention within missional hermeneutics so far. There are at least two additional streams that have been identified as worthy of serious consideration. The first of these, emphasized by James V. Brownson (and identified as the fourth stream in Hunsberger's taxonomy), recognizes the function of the gospel "as an interpretive

20. Barram, *Missional Economics*, 36.

matrix within which the received biblical tradition is brought into critical conversation with a particular human context."[21] As the New Testament authors "draw on elements of prior tradition and bring them into critical relationship with the current moment," they must discern "which parts of the tradition [will be] brought to bear upon which dimensions of the presenting context, and in what particular ways." For Brownson, the gospel serves in these situations as an "inner guidance system, an inner gyroscope" for such discernment.[22]

Brownson is interested in how the apostle Paul and others draw on the gospel as they seek to discern what faithful missional participation would look like in a given context. There are elements here of the first two lenses of biblical interpretation. Historically, we can seek to go *behind the text* in order to explore how the gospel was utilized contextually as a "matrix," by various authors. And from a literary perspective, we recognize that New Testament authors often drew on Old Testament texts. Such intertextuality fits well within a *text itself* framework.

Brownson is also concerned with the same dynamics in the contemporary church today. Hunsberger notes that "what happens in the New Testament . . . is paradigmatic for the daily engagement of the gospel with our own culture or cultures today."[23] Not only does this reflect *behind-the-text*, historical considerations as later generations of Christians seek to apply paradigmatic biblical input in their own times and places, there is also an *in-front-of-the-text* angle at play here as well, inasmuch as readers come to the biblical text from within their cultural contexts and with their located questions. While Brownson's observations have probably not yet received the attention they deserve, his 1998 book, *Speaking the Truth in Love: New Testament Resources for a Missional Hermeneutic*, helpfully unpacks some of the issues.[24] Undoubtedly, future work in missional hermeneutics will need to explore them further.

A fifth stream, also suggested by Brownson, focuses on the importance of God's missional people reading with others who are different. The emphasis here is on real human encounters that foster an overcoming of

---

21. Hunsberger, "Mapping," 59.

22. Hunsberger, "Mapping," 60.

23. Hunsberger, "Mapping," 60.

24. Brownson, *Speaking the Truth in Love*. For an exploration of some of the dynamics implied by the fourth stream, see also Barram, "Fools for the Sake of Christ."

"*indifference*."[25] For Brownson, this would include exploration of cross-cultural experiences within the biblical text, reflecting dynamics both of the *text itself* and what may be *behind it*, but it would also include consideration of the interpretive implications of contemporary engagement with difference for today's readers *in front of the text*. Arguably, in fact, this fifth stream could be considered part of the third (*in front of* the text), though it helpfully extends that stream by flagging the all-too-common tendency of faith communities to become insular and to revel in their relative isolation and uniformity. Brownson's concerns are warranted and important, and we believe our constructive proposal in the second part of the book offers a helpful way of beginning to explore them. Recent work in the Forum on Missional Hermeneutics has increasingly emphasized Brownson's concerns in a variety of ways, and we anticipate that these streams will receive more explicit attention as missional hermeneutics continues to mature.

Addressing the Specter of *Eisegesis*

As with any set of interpretive assumptions, methods, and practices, we tend to find what we are looking for. The questions we ask often determine our results. A certain interpretive circularity is always, therefore, unavoidable. As we have noted, when we approach the Bible from the perspective of missional hermeneutics, we find both divine purposiveness and the participation of God's people in those purposes. And readers in every age and context are themselves effectively invited by these biblical texts to participate in the divine mission. Interpreters are thus invited to engage in the very thing they are exploring.

Traditional historical-critical biblical scholarship has privileged certain assumptions about history, authorship, and textual analysis—and thus, not surprisingly, particular kinds of conclusions in relation to those assumptions. Circularity was, as usual, intrinsic to the process, even if interpreters imagined that they were engaged in fully "objective" inquiry. Concerned to foster accurate, responsible *exegesis* ("leading out" or "drawing out" biblical meaning), historical-critical scholarship fretted deeply about the dangers of *eisegesis* (reading meanings *into* biblical texts that were foreign to them). Again, the traditional, historical-critical assumption was that the intent of

---

25. This quote and the content in this paragraph are drawn from an unpublished response (at the 2008 Annual Meetings of the Society of Biblical Literature) by Brownson to Hunsberger's original paper, "Proposals."

the author (and/or of the editor/s)—that is, the original, intended meaning of a given biblical text—could (at least theoretically) be accurately discerned and articulated by interpreters. Even if the meaning of a particular biblical passage were perceived to be unclear, or if its meaning were debated, historical-critical interpreters assumed that doing more scholarly analysis would, theoretically and eventually, lead to clarity.

Missional hermeneutics intentionally and self-consciously builds upon more recent recognition that being conscious of—and up front about—its located assumptions, presuppositions, and commitments does not, in fact, make research *eisegetical* as much as it simply reflects interpretive honesty. The putative neutrality with which historical-critical interpreters approach texts (ready merely to follow available evidence) is considered to be a hermeneutical virtue ensuring that interpretive processes and products are *exegetical* rather than *eisegetical* in character.[26] Postmodern scholarship, however, rightly rejects such facile notions of interpretive neutrality, recognizing that these traditional assumptions effectively center privileged and dominant voices while doing little to avoid the supposed bogeyman of eisegesis.

Again, postmodernity has conclusively demonstrated that all interpretation is located and perspectival. In other words, no interpretation can claim to be completely objective. All readers—all interpreters—come to the text already situated ("located") in particular contexts, with certain assumptions, preferences, tendencies, interests, commitments, characteristics, experiences, and so forth. Again, therefore, some interpretive circularity is unavoidable: what we look at is always affected by the located perspectives from and through which we view it. Rather than lamenting our human inability to avoid circularity (regardless of what we are attempting to interpret), we can simply acknowledge circularity—which we might describe in terms of *praxis* here—as part of the interpretive process, and recognize that it productively contributes to that process.

Again, the biblical text itself indicates that God is purposive and active. To interpret the Bible from the vantage point of that *missio Dei* is thus *not* to import something foreign into the text, but rather to attend to perhaps its most important and central facet. Beginning the interpretive process from the assumption that the biblical God is engaged in fulfilling

---

26. Simply put, *exegesis* has been understood as discovering and drawing out what is actually *in* a text, whereas *eisegesis* was understood to be the opposite—namely, reading things *into* a text that were never there. The reality is that *exegesis* is never entirely separable from *eisegesis*.

divine purposes is effectively to let Scripture speak on its own terms. Unlike the imported interpretive circularities characteristic of traditional historical-criticism, any circularity in missional hermeneutics is already bidden by the texts themselves.

Conclusion

This brief survey of the various streams and lenses that have come to characterize missional hermeneutics to this point should illustrate that while interpretive attention to mission is *not* an *eisegetical* endeavor, it is also less a matter of exegetical methodology than a posture or approach within which methodological concerns can effectively function. Asking questions related to the purposes of God—and human participation within them—does not mean that missional interpreters avoid or eschew the myriad methods and insights that have shaped and characterized biblical scholarship more generally. Rather, to read Scripture missionally is to approach biblical texts with particular kinds of concerns and questions, utilizing any and all methodologies developed within the three standard lenses of biblical interpretation that may help to illuminate their missional dynamics and unpack their implications for contemporary reading communities. In short, missional hermeneutics does not involve innovative exegetical methods. What is new in this movement is the way in which missionally oriented questions have come to the fore of—and thus shape—the exegetical and interpretative process.

Missional hermeneutics reorients biblical interpretation by focusing on biblical testimony about who God is, what God cares about, and what God is doing in the world—and how human beings are invited to participate in those divine purposes. Scripture's intrinsically formative character is naturally emphasized in this approach. The Bible is always far more than an ancient textual object subject to endless rounds of exegetical archaeology. Perhaps more than anything else, biblical literature shapes reading communities, ancient and contemporary, for their participation in God's purposes—in the *missio Dei*.

Again, we are indebted to many colleagues and friends who have joined us in theorizing and practicing missional hermeneutics over the past two decades, and we anticipate that our account of this emerging subfield of biblical interpretation should be relatively uncontroversial for those who have participated in the conversation. Having said that, we suggest that some of the interpretive implications of the *missio Dei*, biblically understood—and the church's participation in it—can and still need to be taken further. In the next part of the book, we seek to unpack some of those implications and related issues, suggesting a particular vision for missional hermeneutics going forward.

Our approach is not so much to propose another stream of missional hermeneutics as it is to suggest a common *telos* or end to the various interpretive steams in keeping with a particular understanding of the divine purpose, or mission of God. That *telos* might simply defined as liberating love. The love of God expressed and lived out in the world leads to the liberation of all things—human beings, animals, and the whole of the created order—from the powers of sin and death.

The primacy of love in hermeneutics and biblical interpretation has been articulated historically by Augustine of Hippo, who writes of this theme in his classic work, *On Christian Doctrine*: "The fulfillment and end of Scripture is the love of God and neighbor." In the midst of all the diversity of biblical teaching and various approaches to hermeneutics and interpretation, Augustine maintains that the sum and ultimate *telos* of all biblical interpretation is love of God and neighbor: "Whoever, then, thinks that [they understand] the Holy Scriptures, or any part of them, but puts such an interpretation upon them as does not build up this twofold love of God and our neighbor, does not yet understand then as [they] ought."[27] Love is the primary concern in the interpretation of Scripture.

This perspective follows in the tradition of the apostle Paul, who wrote in 1 Cor 13:1–3:

> If I speak in the tongues of humans and of angels but do not have love, I am a noisy gong or a clanging cymbal. And if I have prophetic powers and understand all mysteries and all knowledge and if I have all faith so as to remove mountains but do not have love, I am nothing. If I give away all my possessions and if I hand over my body so that I may boast[a] but do not have love, I gain nothing.

If we interpret and use Scripture in ways that do not lead to the love of God and neighbor, we are not interpreting it properly.

As to the result of this love, we believe liberation is a usefully holistic idea to describe its significance and effects in the world following the description of the great Peruvian theologian Gustavo Gutiérrez. He speaks of liberation in three senses—political, cultural, and spiritual. While these

---

27. Augustine, *On Christian Doctrine*, 532–33.

three are interrelated such that none is present without the others, they are also distinct in their particular focus. Together they are part of a single, all-encompassing salvific process that takes root in temporal political history. Importantly, Gutiérrez makes it clear while the salvific process of God's love *always* has a temporal and political dimension, it is not exhausted by temporal and political concerns. He writes, "We can say that the historical, political liberating event *is* the growth of the Kingdom and *is* a salvific event; but it is not *the* coming of the Kingdom, not *all* of salvation."[28]

We take this to be entirely consistent with inauguration of Jesus's public ministry in Luke 4:18–19, where he reads from the Isaiah scroll, "The Spirit of the Lord is upon me, because he has anointed me to bring good news to the poor. He has sent me to proclaim release to the captives and recovery of sight to the blind, to set free those who are oppressed, to proclaim the year of the Lord's favor." Jesus then announces that the Scripture has been fulfilled (v. 21). This is the public pronouncement of Jesus's mission of liberating love. We believe this should be the *telos* of missional hermeneutics and biblical interpretation.

28. Gutiérrez, *Theology of Liberation*, 176–77.

PART TWO

Toward a Missional Hermeneutic of Liberating Love

Introduction to Part Two

As we noted at the outset, we have two primary goals in this book. The first is simply to offer our readers a helpful introduction to the emergence of missional hermeneutics. The first two chapters served as our attempt to do just that. While one could reasonably outline and analyze the development and interpretive frameworks pertaining to missional hermeneutics in other ways, we anticipate that the introduction we have provided in the first two chapters will be welcomed by colleagues within the movement as a fair, balanced, and essentially noncontroversial treatment of what has taken place to this point.[1] We especially hope that readers new to missional hermeneutics have found in those two chapters an accessible on-ramp to understanding some of the concerns and dynamics involved in this kind of interpretation such that they feel empowered to begin exploring and engaging in missional interpretation themselves. We will return, in the last chapter of the book, to offer some final reflections and, most importantly, a number of specific, interpretive questions that will serve as practical guidance for any readers seeking to begin interpreting Scripture missionally. We hope that these questions will prove to be especially generative for preachers, teachers, and Bible study leaders and participants.

---

1. Readers interested in even more granular data about the emergence of missional hermeneutics are encouraged to consult the appendix, which provides an exhaustive list of session topics, participant information, and paper titles from more than twenty years of conference gatherings.

Our second goal in this book is to offer a new and constructive proposal for an explicitly liberative missional hermeneutics that, for us, even more fully reflects and fosters the two-directional scriptural liberation suggested by the title of the book. In this second part, we humbly offer what we have come to believe is a biblically faithful, albeit challenging and "untamed" vision of God's mission. While we do not equate our perspectives with missional hermeneutics itself—as if we were claiming that our vision for this interpretive posture were the only legitimate possibility going forward—we do offer our proposal as one that we find to be compelling and, ultimately, reflective of the liberative nature of Scripture and the wide and holistic scope of God's mission that it articulates across the canon. Our hope is that whether or not our missional hermeneutics colleagues and readers agree with some or all of our proposal, our honest attempt to articulate a biblically inspired, liberative vision of the divine mission will foster more love, compassion, mercy, shalom, justice, and healthy discussion among all who seek to participate in what God is doing in the world—and that such liberative and life-giving activity will become evident far beyond the community of faith.

As authors, the two of us are friends and colleagues personally engaged in the messiness of the human journey of faith—toddling along, as it were, behind Jesus of Nazareth. While we find ourselves energized, inspired, engaged, and constantly challenged by this enigmatic messiah and the divine mission into which he invites his followers, we acknowledge often feeling disillusioned and even distraught at the state of much of what is happening in the church today, perhaps especially in our own context in the United States. So much of what passes for the good news in many contemporary Christian circles with which we are familiar seems to be anything but liberative and life-giving. As a first-century Jewish prophet, Jesus advocated and embodied wholeness, healing, nonviolence, peacemaking, and liberation from all forms of oppression, whether physical, intellectual, or spiritual. He fostered radical generosity and belonging, turning traditional social tables upside down. He announced and lived into a new reality, in which—despite all appearances to the contrary—anyone and everyone under occupation by human "lords" could begin to experience true liberation as participants in a more real, truly divine reign. And he denounced forms of religiosity and theological system-building that relegated concrete manifestations of love, mercy, and justice to secondary status among the pious. How have we turned *that* Jesus into someone who effectively champions our self-serving perspectives, who blesses our traditional loyalties, who baptizes the worst instincts of our partisan political maneuverings, and who, like us, is adept at finding ever more creative arguments to support the demonization and dehumanization of people we don't want to love?

We come to missional hermeneutics informed and shaped by the liberationist idea that no theologizing is ever merely theoretical, but that theological reflection is always an embodied, located endeavor. As authors, we find ourselves unable to read and interpret Scripture in ways that feel fully relevant and responsible when we fail to attend to what we see happening in the world around us, and, more specifically, in the church itself. We are convinced that reading locatedly is not a bug but rather a feature of healthy biblical interpretation, and in humility we offer our proposal in that spirit. While we are convinced that the vision we propose is both faithful to Scripture and appropriately responsive to realities on the ground, we claim nothing final for or about it. Precisely because theological reflection is ongoing and unfinished, our own perspectives— as important as we may believe they are—represent honest but thoroughly incomplete and partial attempts to wrestle with reality as, together with God's people, we journey together. We hope our readers relish the adventure, as we join one another in following Jesus on the road.

In chapter 3, as a point of entry into our constructive proposal for missional hermeneutics going forward, we will briefly reflect on several ways that we as readers have tended, intentionally or otherwise, to shackle Scripture, keeping it from doing its fullest liberative work in our lives. In these reflections, we are attempting to put our presuppositional cards on the table, so to speak. While there is little here for most biblical scholars and theologians that is new—or even, for that matter, controversial—we recognize that some of the things we discuss may still be unfamiliar to many folks preparing for Christian vocations in our colleges and seminaries, let alone to participants in many local Christian communities. For that reason, we believe that they merit at least some brief attention before we articulate our specific vision for missional hermeneutics.

Chapters 4, 5, and 6 lay out our particular vision for a liberative missional hermeneutics. Chapter 4 begins to explore the character of God's liberating mission. Chapter 5 examines the nature and function of Scripture itself. And chapter 6 considers a range of theological dynamics that intersect with and inform our vision for missional hermeneutics.

The book concludes in chapter 7 with a brief, pragmatic overview of how readers may begin to engage with missional hermeneutics themselves.

CHAPTER 3

How We Shackle Scripture

THE BIBLE SPEAKS TO us in many different ways, meeting us where we are and providing comfort, encouragement, insight, wisdom, challenge, guidance, inspiration, and hope as we journey through life. We read about slaves liberated from Egypt, the freedom to be found in Sabbath rest, and legal protections for the most vulnerable. We discover prophetic indictments against societal injustice, wise counsel for challenging circumstances, and an enigmatic, messianic rabbi who offers a yoke that is easy and light. And we are reminded that faith, hope, and love—along with mercy, forgiveness, justice, and reconciliation—are more significant and powerful than hatred, division, revenge, selfish ambition, social power, and greed.

We noted at the outset that the title of this book, *Liberating Scripture*, represents a double entendre—that while the Bible has great power to liberate, it also needs to be liberated from us. Most readers who come to the Bible find in it at least something that is potentially liberating—including freedom from oppression, forgiveness from sin, and release from all that entraps us as human beings and alienates us from one another, from the world around us, from God, and even from ourselves. Indeed, myriads of us have found ourselves opened up to wonder, forgiveness, joy, and freedom through the spirit of God in our engagement with the Bible. We will return to Scripture's liberative nature later. At this point, though, let us consider the other side of the double entendre implied in the title, *Liberating Scripture*.

As we have already mentioned, we often read and interpret the Bible in ways that actually hinder its liberative potential, even if we do so unintentionally. In fact, we must actively endeavor to unshackle Scripture in order to unpack and experience more fully the liberation that it offers to us.

Let us consider a few illustrative but important examples of areas in which we believe it is necessary to liberate Scripture so that it can do its best work in and among us. We are identifying and reflecting on these particular matters not because they are the only things that could be highlighted—or because we believe that Scripture can be read fruitfully only by those who affirm the same things that we do—but rather because rethinking these matters has proven to be especially significant and liberative for us, both personally and professionally, as we continue to engage Scripture and our lives of faith.

Treating the Bible as a Book of Answers or Rules

As Christians, we can effectively shackle the biblical text by treating the Bible as a kind of encyclopedia or storehouse of information—or as a huge, static collection of moral rules and demands, suggestive of a kind of "game plan" for life. As readers, we naturally come to Scripture with our questions and concerns—including those about God, about the world around us, and about life and how to live it. Of course, it is appropriate to approach the Bible in order to see what it may have in store for us. And yet, as valid as the notion may be that the Bible provides answers for our questions, there can also be some problems with this approach to Scripture.

The Bible is far more than an always-at-the-ready compendium of answers and advice. Indeed, most of the topics we may have questions about are *not even addressed* in the Bible. And, if we're honest, Scripture does *not* always provide clear answers to our questions.

In addition, it is important to recognize that the questions we choose to ask inherently determine the kinds of answers we will find. Inadvertently or otherwise, we limit what Scripture can do to us, for us, and in us when we assume that the questions we ask are the only ones that really matter. While the questions we ask of the Bible are valid and important, Scripture also has many questions for us—and potentially answers, as well—beyond those that we may ever think to ask.

The Bible is far more than an answer book. And while there are certainly laws and moral guidelines in the Scripture, it is by no means primarily about rules and "all the things that we aren't supposed to do."

Ultimately, the Bible must be freed and liberated from the nearly universal readerly tendency to try to tame, control, and exploit it. Scripture is a living and dynamic subject that can engage us even when and where we don't expect or want to be engaged. When we treat the Bible primarily as an answer book that responds to our questions on our terms—or as a foreboding book of rules that primarily tells us what to do and what not to do—we domesticate it and thereby miss much of its life-giving force in our lives. We do not get to control the Bible; it needs to be liberated from our control in order that it may do its full, liberative work in and through us as readers. Simply recognizing that can begin to liberate Scripture from the shackles we place upon it, and, in the process, transform how we read it.

Inerrancy

One of the most common ways in which Scripture has been shackled in recent times is through the notion of biblical inerrancy. A central doctrinal commitment in most Protestant evangelical churches, colleges, and seminaries—as well as one of the doctrinal standards for the Evangelical Theological Society—inerrancy usually means that everything the Bible teaches is historically and factually accurate.

According to the Chicago Statement on Biblical Inerrancy and Hermeneutics, since the Bible is inspired by God who is the "Truth and speaks truth only," it is "God's own Word" and is of "infallible divine authority in all matters upon which it touches." Therefore, "being wholly and verbally God-given, Scripture is without error or fault in all its teaching, no less in what it states about God's acts in creation, about the events of world history, and about its own literary origins under God, than in its witness to God's saving grace in individual lives."[1]

Many interpreters have recognized, however, that inerrancy probably leads to more difficulties than it solves. Biblical texts often seem to point in strikingly different, even opposing directions. In Deut 20:16–18, for example, God's people are exhorted to practice a form of holy war not

---

1. From "A Short Statement" (points 1, 2, and 3) in "The Chicago Statement on Biblical Inerrancy," drafted by the International Council on Biblical Inerrancy in October 1978.

uncommon in the ancient Near East, in which enemies are treated merci-lessly, with homicidal violence—and to do so in obedience to God's will.

> But as for the towns of these peoples that the Lord your God is giv-ing you as an inheritance, you must not let anything that breathes remain alive. Indeed, you shall annihilate them—the Hittites and the Amorites, the Canaanites and the Perizzites, the Hivites and the Jebusites—just as the Lord your God has commanded, so that they may not teach you to do all the abhorrent things that they do for their gods and you thus sin against the Lord your God.

By contrast, other biblical texts in the Hebrew Bible, as well as in the New Testament, suggest that the divine will moves in quite different directions. In the Sermon on the Mount, while Jesus reminds his listeners of the Levitical command to "love [their] neighbor," he goes on to challenge them to "love [their] enemies and pray for those who persecute [them]" (Matt 5:43–44). For his part, Paul encourages his Roman brothers and sisters not to "repay anyone evil for evil" and to "live peaceably with all." Indeed, they are "never [to] avenge [themselves]." And, citing Prov 25:21, the apostle affirms the need to feed hungry enemies and quench their thirst (Rom 12:18–20). Similar examples of biblical texts that seem to be in conflict with one another abound.

If these statements are equally reflective of God's will, how do readers make sense of what appear to be conflicting positions regarding behavior in the world? The contemporary doctrine of inerrancy, in spite of its intentions, leaves readers with puzzling and fairly inflexible interpretive options.

According to the Chicago Statement, "the doctrine of inerrancy has been integral to the Church's faith throughout its history."[2] If inerrancy is taken to mean that the Bible has been believed to be true in some sense, this assertion is fairly accurate. The church, however, has *not* always believed that everything in the Bible is historically and factually accurate.

While ancient Christian luminaries such as Origen, Gregory of Nazian-zus, Ambrose, Augustine, and Gregory the Great all affirmed that Scripture was truthful and without error, they did so with philosophical, hermeneuti-cal, and theological assumptions that allowed them to downplay and even sometimes discount the literal meaning of Scripture in favor of spiritual and allegorical interpretation. It is not uncommon to find early Jewish and Christian writers who denied the literal truth of the command of God to kill everything that breathes and the stories of the Canaanite genocide, believing

2. See Article XVI of the Chicago Statement.

that these passages could not be faithful representations of the God revealed in and by Jesus. Augustine of Hippo famously remarked that he could not have become a Christian until he heard Ambrose of Milan teach the Bible using a spiritual and allegorical form of interpretation.[3]

None of the leaders mentioned here, many of whom were instrumental in the establishment of Christian orthodoxy, would have affirmed the details of inerrancy as they have come to be articulated in the Chicago Statement. Insisting on such modern notions of inerrancy effectively shackles Scripture by imposing standards of interpretation that are foreign to what we find in the Bible itself.

Foundationalism

The modern notion of inerrancy is reflective of a particular form of epistemology known as foundationalism. In its broadest sense, foundationalism is the acknowledgment that not all beliefs are of equal significance as we structure what we know. Some beliefs are more basic or foundational and thus serve to give support to other beliefs that are derived from them. Understood in this way, nearly every thinker is in some sense a foundationalist. In philosophical circles, however, classical foundationalism refers to a much stronger epistemological stance than is entailed in this general observation about how beliefs intersect. In its classic Enlightenment form, foundationalism aims to overcome the uncertainty generated by the tendency of fallible human beings to err and the inevitable disagreements and controversies that follow. A strong foundationalist is convinced that the only way to solve this problem is to find some universal and indubitable means of grounding the entire edifice of human knowledge.

This modern quest for epistemological certitude has its philosophical beginnings in the thought of the philosopher René Descartes. Descartes sought to reconstruct the nature of knowledge by rejecting traditional medieval or pre-modern notions of authority and replacing them with the modern conception of indubitable beliefs that are accessible to all individuals (e.g., "I think, therefore I am"). The goal (and result) of assembling an indubitable foundation is a universal knowledge that transcends time and context. Since Descartes, therefore, ideal human knowledge has tended to emphasize the universal, the general, and the theoretical rather

3. On spiritual interpretation by the figures mentioned here, see Franke, *Ancient Christian Commentary*, xviii–xxvii.

than the local, the particular, and the practical. Foundationalist epistemology became one of the dominant assumptions of intellectual pursuit after the Enlightenment and decisively shaped the cultural discourse and practices of the Western world.[4]

Indeed, in the modern doctrine of inerrancy discussed above, Scripture functions as exactly the sort of strong foundation that the classical foundationalists had envisioned. Scripture becomes the true and sole basis for knowledge on all matters that it touches, equally authoritative on questions of science and history as on spiritual and religious concerns.

Ultimately, this approach suggests that if there is a single error in the Bible, none of it can be trusted; if there is one problem, there may as well be a thousand. This is strong foundationalism in action, even when the term is not explicitly invoked. As with inerrancy, this kind of philosophical position effectively shackles Scripture, imposing assumptions on the text that are foreign to its character and composition.

Theological Systems

We also shackle Scripture when we assume that biblical teaching leads straightforwardly to a unified theological system. Read in this way by different groups of Christians, the Bible has contributed to the development of numerous "systems" of theology. These systems are often mutually exclusive, competing for the title of the one true system of doctrine taught in the Bible. And, once such a system is established, it functions in circular fashion as an interpretive guideline for reading the whole Bible.

An overly systematic approach to theology in relation to the texts of Scripture can lead to sectarianism in the Christian community, as different expressions of the church conclude that they have arrived at the one true system of doctrine. Inevitably, they find themselves in conflict with other traditions that have come to different conclusions. The resulting fragmentation and divisiveness in the church contrasts sharply with the work of the Spirit in promoting unity and solidarity in the church.

While an emphasis on "systematizing" leads to numerous interpretive challenges, the one that is most germane to our concerns in this volume is that it hinders us from attending fully to the unique voices across the biblical canon. If we take the portrait of Jesus and theological

---

4. For a detailed discussion of foundationalism and its influence on theology, see Grenz and Franke, *Beyond Foundationalism*, 3–54.

perspective expressed in John's Gospel as the template for reading Matthew, Mark, and Luke, the distinctive teaching of each of those Synoptic Gospels may be obscured. The early church rejected harmonizing the four Gospels into one account precisely to preserve the distinctive witness of each. Liberating Scripture requires us to let each text speak from its own unique background, assumptions, and perspectives.

From our perspective, while attention to the canonical shape of Scripture is critical, missional hermeneutics should aim to preserve the integrity of each of the biblical texts, allowing their diverse perspectives to speak. In this way, we hope to account for both the diversity of Scripture as well as the diversity of the church throughout history. These differences are manifestations of Christian diversity when addressing common concerns and of the plurality of social and historical situations in which Christian community comes to expression.

We suggest that in order to unshackle Scripture—to allow the biblical texts to speak for themselves—interpreters would do well to let go of the notion that the Bible teaches a single system of theology. In this way, the liberating witness of Scripture will be unleashed more effectively in the church and the world.

In this regard, we find Karl Barth's perspective helpful. Barth resists the systematization of theology because of the ways in which it belies the God to whom it seeks to bear witness—a God who cannot be pinned down and contained in the confines of a human system of thought. Given that interpretive activity is an inherent and unavoidable facet of all Christian faith and discipleship, Barth acknowledges the temptation to construct theological systems. He concludes, however, that we must finally resist this temptation for the sake of our witness to the living God. Barth writes:

> In this [interpretive] work—it cannot be otherwise in view of its object—we have to do with the question of truth. It is, therefore, inevitable that as a whole and in detail the aim must be definiteness and coherence, and it is to be hoped that the definiteness and sequence of the truth will actually be disclosed. But this being the case, is it not also inevitable that "something like a system" will assert itself more or less spontaneously in dogmatic work? Why, then, should a "system" be so utterly abhorrent? If it asserts itself spontaneously in this way, can it not be forgiven? And if so, why should we be frightened away by a law forbidding systems? May it be that a "system" which asserts itself spontaneously (not as a system, but as a striving for definiteness and coherence) signifies

obedience and is therefore a shadow of the truth? It may well be so. But even in this case the danger is still there. The fact that unauthorised systematisation may be forgiven does not mean that the tendency to systematisation is authorised. Nor does the fact that even in the fatal form of an intrinsically unauthorised systematisation true obedience may finally be demonstrated and a shadow of the truth disclosed.[5]

The missional hermeneutics we will propose follows Barth's nuanced perspective for the sake of our witness to God and God's mission in the world, but also in order to allow the texts of Scripture to speak as witnesses to the purposes of God and God's dream for the world—even in ways that may challenge or deepen our theological commitments.

Ignoring Genre

The Bible is not really a single book. Rather, it is a large collection—an anthology, really—of quite diverse documents that together make up what we call the biblical canon. Among other things, there are creation accounts, genealogies, epic familial stories, complex law codes, narratives about Israel's development and monarchical rulers, prophetic statements, compilations of wisdom, musical and lyrical poetry, stories about the ministry, death, and resurrection of a rabbi named Jesus, an account of some crucial events in the life of the earliest church, letters of widely varied length and character, and apocalyptically oriented visions and exhortation. Within this literature, we find historical memory, communal instruction, and moral formation—as well as encouragement, humor, indictment, aphoristic and speculative wisdom, hope, consolation, lament, metaphor, parable, and more. In order to interpret these texts responsibly and not entirely according to our own assumptions and proclivities, we must take their literary genres seriously.

The two creation accounts (Gen 1:1—2:4a; 2:4b—3:24) are quite different from one another, and they both differ radically from law codes, gospels, and the Pauline letters. We should not expect the same type of information from each of these kinds of literature, any more than we should expect the same thing from a stand-up comedy routine and a dramatic television miniseries. Ancient authors and audiences would have been far more familiar with the various genres that we find in biblical literature than we are. When we read the creation stories in Genesis looking

5. Barth, *Church Dogmatics* 1/2, 868–67.

for scientific data, or peruse the book of Job anticipating a straightforward historical biography of a Middle Eastern man, or claim to read "as fact" something in the Bible that its author intended metaphorically, we *literally* misread the texts. We must be humble enough and responsible enough to read biblical literature in ways that respect its own forms of communicating, recognizing that just as we communicate different kinds of things today through different genres, so does the Bible. Many *claim* to read Scripture *literally*, but when we ignore genre we end up reading not what the text actually says but rather what we assume it does. Biblical literalism effectively shackles and does violence to the Bible by disregarding genre, effectively leading us to misread Scripture.[6] In short, disregard for biblical genre amounts to a form of human control over the Bible—a shackling of Scripture from which it must be liberated.[7]

6. Richard Rohr's comments (*Jesus' Plan*, viii) nearly a quarter-century ago are instructive, particularly with regard to the continued emergence and influence of fundamentalism, which ignores genre:

> Every indication is that the growing phenomenon in our society will be fundamentalism. Fundamentalism refuses to listen to what the Gospel authors are really saying to their communities. It enters into a nonhistorical love affair with words—I don't know how else to describe it. The human need for clarity and certitude leads fundamentalists to use sacred writings in a mechanical, closed-ended and authoritarian manner. This invariably leaves them trapped in their own cultural moment in history, and they often totally miss the real message along with the deepest challenges and consolations of Scripture.
>
> In the name of taking the word literally, the fundamentalist is in fact missing the literal word. Isn't that ironic? The real meaning of the text is largely missed by people who say that they take it all literally. In other words, the metaphorical sense, the mythological sense, the sense of religious psychology and sacred story is in fact the *literal*, real sense—just as it is when you and I talk, write and communicate with each other.
>
> . . . Religion has always needed the language of metaphor, symbol, story and analogy to point to the transcendent universe. There is actually no other way. Against conventional wisdom, such usage does not demand less of us but much more. Maybe that is why we so consistently avoid sacred story in favor of mere mechanical readings that we can limit and control.

7. It is also worth noting that "truth" is *not* a literary genre. While Scripture undoubtedly communicates truth, we should not assume that everything in the Bible is equally true or that everything it says is true in exactly the same ways.

Ignoring Context

Relatedly, we must take context seriously as we interpret the Bible. Too often, intentionally or not, we shackle Scripture by utilizing (and often weaponizing) portions of the biblical text without adequate regard for the sociocultural, historical, literary, and argumentative contexts in which those passages were and are embedded. The context in which the word "love" is used matters tremendously: love can mean quite different things depending on whether one uses it in reference to a spouse, a child, a pet, a poem, a nation, or ice cream. Linguistically, words and phrases do not simply and definitively "mean" things in isolation; rather, they connote particular kinds of things when used in different contexts.

In the same way that property investors and realtors often tout the importance of "location, location, location," biblical interpreters have regularly highlighted the significance of "context, context, context." Attention to the who, what, when, where, why, and how of a given scriptural passage helps us avoid making the text say what we want it to say. Prooftexting—that is, lifting a biblical passage out of context to prove a point—is one particular way in which readers can shackle (and potentially weaponize) Scripture.

Ignoring What We Bring to the Text

We never come to the Bible entirely empty-handed, or as blank slates. We *always* bring our own characteristics, identities, perspectives, interpretive frameworks, experiences, roles and statuses, proclivities, biases, theological commitments and loyalties—and so much more—into our reading and interpretation of the Bible. We bring ourselves and who we have become into the interpretive process. Much of what we see in the Bible is what we are already conditioned by our experiences and identities to see. This makes it absolutely crucial that we listen to and learn from the perspectives of others as we explore and engage Scripture. No one of us "gets" the entire picture alone. We need each other. Diversity is a gift from God, and only together, in community, do we have the opportunity to hear and engage the text more fully than we otherwise would on our own.

Obviously, this is true with regard to our experiences with gender. But it is equally true with regard to other aspects of our lives, including race and ethnicity; socioeconomic class and status; cultural characteristics; political perspectives; theological presuppositions and denominational commitments; family, education, and work experiences; and so forth. Each of these factors—and so much more about us—goes into the process of interpretation. Indeed, our identities and collected experiences are never entirely static as we continue to live and grow and experience new things all the time. Again, we cannot and should not pretend that these factors are unimportant, incidental, or irrelevant facets and characteristics of our lives. These things matter as we interpret. We may need to let go of some of our perspectives and commitments as we get deeper into the process of interpretation, when we learn that our own views and biases are limited. But we always have the opportunity to come to the text humbly and honestly, recognizing that we and our perspectives are limited—and doing so is a tremendous first step in liberating Scripture so that it may continue to foster our own liberation.

Conclusion

It is ironic, but nonetheless true: the Bible itself needs to be liberated from our tendencies to control it. Indeed, the more we learn to "liberate" the Bible, the more fully we can experience the liberation it seeks to offer to us. In this regard, we believe that the kind of missional hermeneutics that we seek to articulate in this book can be a real game changer.

In the next three chapters, we lay out a proposal for a particular kind of liberative missional hermeneutics, one that we hope will further the discussion of this interpretive posture in both important and healthy ways. As authors, we are less concerned with being innovative or "right" than with seeking both to inspire and model the kinds of multivocal and generous conversation that we believe faithful participation in God's liberative mission necessitates. In the next chapter, we begin to consider the nature of that divine mission.

CHAPTER 4

Toward a Vision of the *Missio Dei*

IN SPITE OF THE consensus within *missio Dei* theology that God, by God's very nature, is a missional God, and that the church of this missional God must therefore be a missional church, other elements have been contested. Two of the most significant—the precise nature of that divine mission and the nature of the church's participation in it—continue to be discussed and debated. Such matters invite and require interpretation—and are always shaped by theological and hermeneutical commitments.

Below, we begin to offer our interpretation of the mission of God and the role of the church in that mission—recognizing that our construal, like all such enterprises, is necessarily incomplete, tentative, and open to critique. As scholars and people of faith, we embrace the kinds of dialogical approaches to biblical and theological reflection so well embodied in the Jewish tradition, in which honest, vigorous, collaborative, and perpetually ongoing discussion is arguably more important than the assumption that we will ever settle on a final, correct, and entirely defensible proposal for anything related to God or the Bible. Indeed, any presumption of completeness and finality in this regard would have more to do with the human proclivity to idolatry than to an actual appropriation of the divine. Thus, the hermeneutical and theological task always involves seeking to propose ever more responsible and responsive ways of understanding mission in light of the biblical witness and the realities around us today. Again, all interpretation is shaped by the frameworks and lenses that we bring with us, whether explicitly or implicitly. So, what we intend to do here is make explicit a conception of the mission of God that underlies our particular understanding of and proposal for missional hermeneutics.

The Eternal Mission of God

While the mission of God is complex and multifaceted, its central character from which all other aspects flow is love. The idea that God is love is surely one of the most common assumptions of Christians concerning the character of God. This assertion is found repeatedly in the Bible and has been regularly affirmed throughout the history of the church. When we affirm with Scripture and the Christian tradition that God is love, we are affirming something about the very nature of God's being and actions. God is love for all time—past, present, and future—because God lives eternally in the communal fellowship between Father, Son, and Holy Spirit as they participate in the giving, receiving, and sharing of love.

In addition to the affirmations of the centrality of love found in Scripture, the assertion that God is love also finds its basis in Christian theological thinking on the Trinity. While the idea of God as Trinity is often viewed as a doctrinal abstraction, closer consideration reveals that it is in fact central to the notion that God is love.

The close relationship between Father, Son, and Spirit, as well as the distinctions among them, are already evident in the summary formulations found in the New Testament, such as Matt 28:19: "Therefore go and make disciples of all the nations, baptizing them in the name of the Father and of the Son and of the Holy Spirit"; and 2 Cor 13:14: "May the grace of the Lord Jesus Christ, and the love of God, and the fellowship of the Holy Spirit be with you all." The challenge of integrating the twin commitments of oneness and distinction among the persons of the Trinity has led to an emphasis on both the unity and the differentiated plurality of God.

Throughout the history of the church, the affirmation of the triune character of the divine has served to provide a framework for Christian thinking about God and the ongoing development of trinitarian theology. The biblical witness to the experience of the early Christian community with God points beyond this temporal encounter to the eternal life of God. In addition to acting in the history of the world, the Bible pictures God as having a history in which creation is not the beginning point, but rather a particular event in the continuing story of the divine life that stretches from the eternal past into the eternal future.

While the acts of God in history provide the basis for speaking of the doctrine of the Trinity, they are also indicative of God's ongoing internal life, and Scripture invites us to think through the implications of this history with respect to the character of God. The self-revelation of God reflects the character of God. The revelation of God in Jesus Christ is the living embodiment and exposition of God's gracious character in relation to humanity as the One who loves.

God's love for the world is not that of an impassable Deity, but rather that of one who is actively and passionately involved in the ongoing drama of life in the world. The love of God for the created order revealed in Jesus Christ points us to the internal life of God as an eternal, trinitarian fellowship of love shared between Father, Son, and Holy Spirit. In other words, explication of the triune God in God's self-disclosure in and to creation is at the same time the explication of the triune God in the divine reality. In summarizing this story, the Christian tradition affirms that from all eternity past and into the eternal future, God has been and will be in an active loving relationship characterized by the giving, receiving, and sharing of love between Father, Son, and Holy Spirit.

This relationship includes both difference and unity. This eternal fellowship of divine love is characterized by both unity-in-plurality and plurality-in-unity such that we affirm that the one God exists in three distinct persons (to use the classical language): Father, Son, and Holy Spirit—and that the three together are the one God. This means that difference and otherness are part of the divine life throughout eternity. While Father, Son, and Holy Spirit together are one God, their unity is not an outgrowth of sameness. Rather, they are one in the very midst of their difference.

The relationality of the life of God brings us back to the affirmation that God is love. Articulating the doctrine of the Trinity in accordance with the category of relationality gives us an indication as to how this biblical and classical assertion about love is to be comprehended. From the beginning and throughout all of eternity, the life of the triune God has been and continues to be characterized by love. In addition to enjoying the support of the biblical witness and the tradition of the church, love is an especially fruitful term for comprehending the life of God since it is an inherently relational concept. Love requires both subject and object. Because God is a triune plurality-in-unity and unity-in-plurality, God comprehends both love's subject and love's object. For this reason, when viewed theologically, the statement "God is love" refers primarily to the eternal, relational intra-trinitarian fellowship among Father, Son and Holy Spirit.

The interdependent relationality of the divine life, coupled with the presence of difference and otherness, leads to the conclusion that the love of God is not an assimilating love. This love does not seek to make that which is different the same. Rather, God lives in harmonious fellowship with the other through the active relations of self-sacrificing, self-giving love.

This eternal mission has its origin in the life of God, who from all eternity has been in an active relationship involving the giving, receiving, and sharing of love between Father, Son, and Holy Spirit. In the words of David Bosch, "God is the fountain of sending love. This is the deepest source of mission. It is impossible to penetrate deeper still."[1] There is mission because God loves. The love that characterizes the mission of God from all eternity is the compelling basis for the extension of the divine mission to the world.

The Temporal Mission of God

From the perspective of the eternal mission of God, creation can be understood as a reflection of the expansive love of God, whereby the triune God brings into being another reality, that which is not God, and establishes a relationship of love, grace, and blessing for the purpose of drawing that reality into participation in the divine fellowship of love. In this way the love of God is expanded beyond Father, Son, and Holy Spirit to include others.

Human beings, created in the image of God, rebel, however, against the love of God and others. Instead of seeking the well-being of their fellow humans and the created order, they have continued to seek their own good at the expense of others, establishing oppressive societies that colonize and marginalize their citizens, particularly the powerless and vulnerable. This rebellion, along with the dispositions of the intellect, emotions, and will that bring it into fruition, is what Scripture calls sin. The result is enmity among the peoples of the earth.

In response to this situation, Jesus called the world to follow his way of life and participate in the reign of God, a community of love in which everyone has enough and no one needs to be afraid. The Spirit is sent into the world to call, guide, and empower the community of Christ's followers in their missional vocation to be the people of God in the particular social,

1. Bosch, *Transforming Mission*, 392.

historical, and cultural circumstances in which they are situated. Through the witness of the church to the good news of God's love and mission, the Spirit calls forth a new community from every tribe and nation, centered on Jesus Christ, to be a provisional demonstration of God's will for all creation and empowers it to live God's love for the sake of the world.

This missional pattern, manifested in the world through the sending of the Son and the sending of the Spirit out of love for the world, is lived out and expressed in the context of the eternal community of love and points to the missional character of God who seeks to extend the love shared by Father, Son, and Holy Spirit into the created order. Flowing out of the divine life in Trinity, love is central to the mission of God in the world. As an out-working of divine love, the mission of God is expressed in the world through the life of Jesus and the witness of the Spirit as salvation.

This salvation entails the complete liberation of the created order—humanity and the entire cosmos—from the powers of sin and death. When speaking of salvation, it is important not to understand it from the individualistic perspective of modern Western culture. From that per-spective, salvation has often been viewed primarily as the redemption of particular individuals for a heavenly future. To read the biblical witness in this way is to miss the full scope and grandeur of the divine mission. God's actions are on behalf of the whole created order so that it will be set free from its bondage to decay.

Ephesians 2 articulates the consequences of the work of God in Christ to bring reconciliation between Jew and gentile, and therefore, the world. Peace and harmony in the world is central to the mission of God. According to the New Testament, the divine mission of peace promises harmony between Jew and gentile; even now, at the outset of the third millennium, that same mission necessitates peace among the religions of the world. Apart from such religious peace, there is no hope for the salvific peace that God intends for the world.

The good news of the gospel is peace in the world and the end of the violence and hostility that destroys life and leads to death. This is a funda-mental part of the message of salvation. The language of the New Testament uses a range of words, images, and phrases to articulate a comprehensive vision of God's mission of salvation, including liberation, transformation, new creation, peace, reconciliation, and justification.[2] This salvific mission is rooted in the self-giving, self-sacrificing love of God expressed in the eternal

2. Gorman, *Becoming the Gospel*, 25.

trinitarian fellowship and made known in the created order through the life, death, and resurrection of Jesus Christ. It is this divine mission that forms the context for an understanding of the mission of the church.

The Mission of the Church

Missionary theologian Lesslie Newbigin has articulated the centrality of Christian congregational formation for the work of God in the world, suggesting that the church is the primary reality that needs to be accounted for and developed if we are to see a demonstrable Christian impact on public life in an increasingly secular world. In making this assertion, Newbigin does not discount the importance of the numerous public activities in which Christians engage with the claims and implications of the gospel—such as special events, conferences, evangelistic work, and the distribution of Bibles and Christian literature. While these activities are significant and worthwhile, he maintains that they are ultimately of secondary importance—and only have power to accomplish the purposes for which they are intended as they arise from, are firmly rooted in, and lead inextricably back to a believing community. He writes:

> How is it possible that the gospel should be credible, that people should come to believe that the power which has the last word in human affairs is represented by a man hanging on a cross? I am suggesting that the only answer, the only hermeneutic of the gospel, is a congregation of men and women who believe it and live by it.[3]

This type of all-encompassing, interdependent, individual and communal formation is precisely what is understood in the New Testament as participation in the mission of God. It is discipleship in the way of Jesus that has the capacity to change the world and bring about God's purposes. This kind of formation is a slow process, however, one that requires longstanding faithfulness in the face of difficult and seemingly insurmountable circumstances.

David Bosch concludes that the comprehensive nature of the divine mission demands a more integral and holistic understanding of the character of salvation and therefore, the mission of the church, than has traditionally been the case: "Salvation is as coherent, broad, and deep as the

---

3. Newbigin, *Gospel in a Pluralist Society*, 227.

needs and exigencies of human existence. Mission therefore means being involved in the ongoing dialogue between God, who offers salvation, and the world, which—enmeshed in all kinds of evil—craves that salvation."[4] It is this divine mission that shapes the vocation of the church sent into the world to continue the work of Jesus. As he was sent, so he sends the church (John 20:21).

The extension of the mission of God into the created order occurs not only through the sending of the Son and the Spirit, but also in the sending of the church. As Bosch observes, this biblical pattern demonstrates that mission is derived from the very nature of God and must be situated in the context of the doctrine of the Trinity rather than ecclesiology or soteriology. From this perspective, the classical doctrine of the *missio Dei*—expressed as God the Father sending the Son, and the Father and the Son sending the Spirit—may be expanded "to include yet another 'movement': Father, Son, and Spirit sending the church into the world."[5]

The church is a movement sent into the world by God through Jesus Christ to live out in its own life the gift of God's peace in the world. The church is therefore not simply to proclaim the reign of God but to bear in its own life the reality and presence of that reign in the midst of the present world. Hence, the mission of the church encompasses both the character of its internal communal life as well as its external activities in the world.

From this perspective, the gospel is both a message to be proclaimed as well as a way of life. As a message to be proclaimed, the gospel is the good news that in Jesus Christ, God is liberating the world from the powers of sin and death and reconciling human beings with God, each other, and the whole of creation in order to establish *shalom* in the cosmos. As a way of life in the world, the community provisionally demonstrates the announced reality of the gospel in the present even as it anticipates its coming eschatological fullness. The church is the gathered community of the followers of Jesus Christ who believe in this good news and are prepared to live by it. This community is sent into the world by the triune God for the purpose of bearing witness to the gospel as a sign, instrument, and foretaste of the kingdom of God.

The church is called to bear God's image as a sign of the kingdom of God, a visible community that bears in its own life the presence of God's coming reign. This notion is connected with the idea that human beings

4. Bosch, *Transforming Mission*, 400.
5. Bosch, *Transforming Mission*, 390.

are created in the image of God. It is important to remember, however, that this assertion is both an ontological status and a vocational calling, a destiny toward which human beings are moving. Being in the image of God is not simply a status or condition, but is rather a movement with a goal, that of bearing God's image in the world.

Viewing the image of God as connected to our divinely given calling to represent God means that all persons are made in God's image and that all are called to share in the human vocation of reflecting the loving care of God to creation. In the face of human rebellion against this vocational calling, Jesus is sent to bear this image as the clear representation of the character of God in the world (2 Cor 4:4–6; Col 1:15) and to call forth a community to follow him in bearing this image in the world. Those who follow this path are united to Christ and share in his role as the image of God.

Indeed, the entire biblical panorama may be read as reflecting the divine purpose of bringing into being a people who reflect the divine character and thus fulfill their vocational calling as image bearers of God. Following the pattern of Jesus, the church proclaims the gospel of the kingdom and God's love for all people. It calls on those who hear this good news to repent and become disciples of Jesus, initiating a new way of life in the world, leading to the formation of a new community—a welcoming and inclusive community that lives the love of God for the world and transcends the divisions that are so often used to exclude people from the blessing and peace of God's kingdom.

In the letter to the Galatians, Paul summarizes the significance of the gospel for the divisions that destroy the peace and harmony God intends for creation (3:28): "There is neither Jew nor Gentile, neither slave nor free, nor is there male and female, for you are all one in Christ Jesus." This succinct summary can be extended to all other social bifurcations that human beings can dream up that divide people from each other and imply, directly or indirectly, that some don't belong and can't participate in the new humanity made possible through Jesus Christ. As the church pursues and embodies this inclusive vision of new community in the way of Jesus, it bears the image of God as a sign of God's kingdom.

The church is also called by Jesus to continue his work as an instrument of the kingdom in the power of the Spirit. While it is certainly true that God is at work outside of the church, the New Testament characterization of the church as the body of Christ leads to the conclusion that it is intended to be a focal point of the mission of God in the world, shaped by the mission and ministry of Jesus.

The emphasis throughout the Gospels is on the liberation of people from the powers of sin and death. This suggests an understanding of the church as the community of Christ's followers who join with Jesus in his struggle for the emancipation of humanity and, indeed, all of creation, from these forces of evil. The mission of the church, in keeping with the mission of Jesus, is to proclaim and live out the pattern of God's liberating activity so that those who live under the oppressive powers of this world will see that their deliverance and freedom from these circumstances is a central element of the gospel and the mission of God in the world.

The particular concern for the poor and marginalized is powerfully expressed in Matt 25:31–46, which depicts those who inherit the kingdom of God as people who feed the hungry, offer the thirsty something to drink, welcome the stranger, provide clothing for the naked, take care of the sick, and visit those in prison. Texts like this—and there are many others—demonstrate the calling of the church to participate in the temporal, here-and-now activity of social ministry as basic to the mission of the church as it follows Jesus.

The social concreteness of the Gospel narratives points beyond common interpretations that construe the activity of deliverance and freedom from the power of sin in primarily, or only, a spiritual sense. Embedded in the Jewish tradition, the vision of emancipatory change is to be enacted in the present in such a way that the existing social order is actually altered. Gospel-shaped liberation is holistic and encompasses not only the spiritual, but the cultural and political as well. Together, they are part of a single, all-encompassing process that takes root in temporal history and grows into the world intended by God. This is the notion of salvation envisioned in Scripture. The church is sent into the world to participate in this historical process as it continues the work of the kingdom initiated by Jesus.

In addition to its calling to be a sign and instrument of the kingdom of God, the church is also called to be the dwelling place of the Spirit as a foretaste of that kingdom. The Spirit is given to the church to empower it for participation in God's mission as a new community that transcends the divisions that so easily divide and cause hostility and suspicion among human beings made in God's image.

A central feature of this new community gathered together in the name of Jesus is corporate worship. In the worship of God, the community comes together as one body and declares its adoration of God and thankfulness for the gifts of faith, hope, and love—as well as its dependence on God for its witness in the world. Worship is a central element of the witness of the church to the reign of God in the world. As the church gathers together in worship, we celebrate God's presence, share concerns, pray, and seek the strength to continue on in faithful witness. As such, worship is a fundamental expression of the mission of the church and not an activity separate from that mission.

Through a new life together of interdependent relationality and corporate worship, the church bears witness to a new world that finds its coherence in the love of God revealed in Jesus Christ and attested by the power of the Spirit. This communal form of life is a foretaste of the world as it is willed to be by God. The world as God wills it to be is not a present reality, but rather lies in the eschatological future. Hence, Jesus taught his disciples to pray, "Your kingdom come. Your will be done, on earth as it is in heaven" (Matt 6:9–10). This is a prayer to bring into being a new reality, when God will put everything right and order the cosmos in accordance with the intentions of creation.

— CHAPTER 5 —

The Liberating Word

THROUGHOUT THE BIBLE, WE read of people who are convinced that God intends to bring about a world in which humans and all of creation may flourish, and, to that end, God establishes a community that is to be characterized by love, joy, and peace. We might say that the divine intent in creation is to bring about a world in which, ultimately, everyone has enough and no one needs to be afraid. Human beings, however, rebelled against this purpose. Instead of seeking the well-being of their fellow humans, they sought their own good at the expense of others. This established oppressive societies that colonized and marginalized the vast majority of people, particularly the powerless and vulnerable. Such communities—characterized by political repression, economic exploitation, and chronic violence—were characteristic of the ancient Near East and the Roman Empire, and they form the backdrop to the writings of Scripture.

In order to achieve God's creative purpose in a world characterized by domination, liberation is necessary. We see this in the Exodus narrative of Israel's liberation from Egyptian bondage. We see this divine purpose in the exhortation of the prophets that Israel should not follow the oppressive patterns of other societies. We see this is the announcement of Jesus, citing Isaiah, concerning his public ministry in Luke 4:18–21: "The Spirit of the Lord is upon me, because he has anointed me, to bring good news to the poor. He has sent me to proclaim release to the captives and recovery of sight to the blind, to set free those who are oppressed, to proclaim the year of the Lord's favor." As we mentioned in the previous chapter, the vast majority of Christians affirm that the Bible is in some sense the word of God. As such, we would expect it to function as an instrument of liberation in keeping with the purposes of God.

Tragically, this has not been the case all too often. Scripture has been used again and again throughout history as a justification for oppression, slavery, and even extermination. It is in this context that an understanding of the ways in which Scripture is understood to be the word of God becomes crucially important.

We have discussed the problem of ignoring genre when we engage biblical literature. One consequence of this problem is that we tend to read all biblical texts and themes as being of equal importance. From such a perspective, the Canaanite genocide is understood to have the same relative value as the Ten Commandments, Psalm 23, or the Sermon on the Mount. In addition, an understanding of the Bible as the word of God that sees it all as coming directly from the voice of God misses the human dimension of Scripture's production and thereby enshrines the cultural assumptions of the ancient writers as normative for all times. From this perspective, the oppressive patriarchy that was assumed by the cultures in which the texts of Scripture were written is taken to be of divine origin since it colors all of the biblical texts. Sadly, this view has shaped the entire history of the church, to its detriment. The failure to appreciate the contextual nature of the texts themselves has locked biblical interpretation into particular cultural molds and obscured the liberating intentions of Scripture.

From our perspective, missional hermeneutics must seek to liberate Scripture from the shackles of many of the traditional forms and assumptions of biblical interpretation in order to unleash its liberative intentions. We propose that this begins with a more theologically nuanced understanding of the idea that Scripture is the word of God.

If our experience is anything close to typical, when most Christians hear the phrase "the word of God," they immediately think of the Bible— and only the Bible. This is perhaps understandable given the number of times they hear preachers and teachers refer to the Bible as the word of God. The danger in this is that they then assume that the word of God refers to a past action that is now contained in the Bible. It also leads to the conclusion that if we want to gain knowledge of the divine perspective on any question, we simply turn to the Bible to discover what is to be found in its ancient pages. In this way, the Bible comes to be viewed as an object that can be pinned down for study, dissection, and scrutiny in order to discover God's purpose and intentions. And in fact it has often been treated in just this way.

Based on the witness of the Bible itself, however, things appear to be more dynamic and complex. The epistle to the Hebrews depicts the word of God as "living and active" (Heb 4:12), suggesting that the word of God is an ongoing, vibrant reality that cannot be corralled, contained, or controlled. This leads to a different way of thinking about the word of God.

The Word of God in Three Forms

In order to capture a more dynamic understanding, we suggest, along with many others, that the word of God is best understood as an action of God— or as an ongoing event—in which God has spoken, speaks, and will speak in ways that are consistent with God's purposes for creation. It is always past, present, and future. From this perspective, we encounter and engage this divine act or event through the Spirit-inspired and Spirit-guided means of Scripture and its proclamation in the life of the church.

What is particularly significant about this understanding of the word of God is that since it is *God's* word and not ours, it is never available to us in a direct, straightforward way. It cannot therefore be properly conceived of as a deposit of divine truth from which the church and human beings can draw eternally stable conclusions about God and the world, or a set of propositional statements that can be consulted for timeless information about the divine.

To view it in this fashion would be to suggest that we can gain control over the word of God and press it into the service of our own particular agendas and concerns. In other words, we shackle it and use it for our own ends. In the history of the church, the Bible has sadly been weaponized and used against others who did not share the commitments of those with ecclesial and cultural power. Scripture needs to be liberated from this sort of usage in order that it might be the liberating word it is intended to be.

In order to assist in the establishment of a more dynamic conception of the word of God, we suggest, following theologians such as Karl Barth, a threefold understanding: the act of revelation itself; the Spirit-inspired attestation and witness to revelation in the words of the prophets and the apostles contained in Scripture; and the proclamation of that witness in the communities who believe it and are committed to following it.

In seeking to explain this event, we might imagine three concentric circles that represent three movements in the communication and reception of the word of God. The innermost circle of the three would be the word of God as revelation or self-revelation. This is the divine speech and action authored and spoken by God for the purpose of establishing a relationship with us and making God's intentions known.

This revelation is represented to us and made expressible and approachable through the human speech and actions found in both Scripture and the proclamation of the church. These form two additional circles in the event of the word of God. The human words of Scripture and proclamation are intended by God to be the bearers and witnesses of God's divine self-revelation to human beings in diverse historical and cultural situations. Hence, the word of God may be described as the word revealed, the word written, and the word proclaimed.

Another way to picture this event is to imagine a stone cast into the water with rippling effects that go on and on throughout time and into eternity. God speaks and acts (revelation), humans receive God's speech-acts and bear witness to them in the written word (Scripture), and they continue to interpret and tell of them in the spoken word (proclamation). As the word of God is encountered by human beings throughout history in revelation, Scripture, and proclamation, the expansive goodness of God's love and grace is ever more fully known in the human experience, as are the challenges of faithful participation in God's purposes for creation.

One of the important elements of this conception of the word of God is its human dimension. Human beings participate at every stage of the unfolding of the word of God—as those who receive God's self-revelation, bear witness to it through interpretation and preservation in the texts of Scripture, and continue its expansion through the act of proclamation. In this conception, Scripture stands as the central nexus point between the self-revelation of God and the proclamation of that revelation in the witness of the church.

Revelation and Scripture

In order to conceptualize Scripture as a form of the word of God, we must begin with the idea of revelation. How are we able to know anything about the being and character of God, or about the mission of that God in the world? The Christian answer to this question starts with the notion of revelation. Christian teaching on revelation is rooted in the conviction that God speaks in order to establish a connection with us and provide guidance and direction concerning the conduct of our lives. The purpose of this divine speech, according to the Christian tradition, is to draw creatures into relationship with their creator, inviting them to share in the love of God and to participate in God's purposes.

For Christians, the preeminent act of revelation occurs in Jesus Christ. One of the implications of this is the priority given to the life and teaching of Jesus in understanding the purposes of God in the world. This is one of the central conclusions of the event of the Transfiguration in Matthew, Mark, and Luke.

In these stories (see Matt 17; Mark 9; Luke 9), Jesus undergoes a metamorphosis, a transformation that results in a significantly altered appearance as he experiences a moment of divine radiance. In addition, Peter, James, and John see Jesus talking with Moses and Elijah. Peter is so amazed that he proposes making three dwellings, one each for Jesus, Moses, and Elijah. Imagine his surprise when a cloud envelopes the group and a voice says, "This is my Son, my beloved; listen to him!" Then Moses and Elijah are gone and Jesus is found alone. For Christians, Jesus is the revelation of God in human form.

Here, it is worth noting the close connection between the teaching of Jesus and the Jewish traditions contained in Scripture. While Jesus is viewed as the preeminent revelation of God, the portrayal of his teachings in the Gospels makes it clear that he is in continuity with the teaching of the law and the prophets and their vision for a world where the will of God is done on earth as it is in heaven. The ways in which the life and teaching of Jesus have been used in the development of anti-Semitism is one of the great tragedies of the Christian tradition. In thinking about Jesus as the revelatory embodiment of God and God's purposes in the world, we must challenge the ways that Christianity became a religion *about* Jesus that was turned against Judaism, rather than the religion *of* Jesus, rooted as it was in the Jewish tradition.

In spite of the importance of revelation in learning about the intentions of God in and for the world, the story does not end here. The reason for this is that revelation is communicated and received by finite human beings who are thoroughly situated in particular locations and contexts that shape their ways of looking at and interpreting the world. Further, the Judeo-Christian understanding of God as infinite has implications for the human understanding of divine truth since that which is finite cannot comprehend the infinite.

Revelation does not provide human beings with a knowledge that directly corresponds to the knowledge of God. The difference between the infinite God and finite human beings suggests the accommodated and mediated character of all human knowledge of God. In other words, human beings can't handle the truth about God as it is in itself. Therefore, because God desires to establish a relationship with us, God accommodates revelation to our limitations so that we can understand God's intentions for us. The notion of divine accommodation and human reception in the self-revelation of God suggests that, in fulfilling its purpose to form communities that participate in the mission of God, revelation is pragmatic. Its intention is to lead us in the right direction, rather than to provide precise information concerning the questions we have about the nature of God and the minute details of philosophy, theology, and metaphysics.

Here is where Scripture comes into the picture. The texts of the Bible are a diverse collection of witnesses to the revelation of God, arising from different social situations and reflecting the perspectives of their authors. Indeed, as we have noted earlier, the Bible is not a single book. Reading it as such will lead to distortions in the interpretation of its varying documents as readers attempt to impose a harmony among the texts. As texts written from different settings and perspectives, each of the voices represented in the canonical collection maintains a distinct point of view that emerges from a particular time and place. The Bible is polyphonic, made up of many voices. Embracing this plurality is one of the most fundamental ways in which we need to liberate Scripture so it can liberate us. And this polyphonic character of Scripture has considerable significance for the relationship between the Bible and church proclamation.

The accommodated self-revelation of God is received in a plurality of cultural settings, and is expressed and proclaimed from these diverse contexts to others over the course of changing social and historical contexts. Scripture paradigmatically reflects these shifting social conditions and circumstances in the diversity of its forms and teachings. From the perspective described here, the relationship between Scripture and revelation means that the Bible is the constitutive and normative witness for the formation and proclamation of Christian communities. At the same time, the relationship between Scripture and Christian proclamation points to the ways in which the texts of Scripture are also the first in an ever-expanding series of presentations of Christian faith throughout history.

Scripture and Christian Proclamation

The ever-expanding series of witnesses to Christian faith in the proclamation of the church constitutes the living tradition of the church. The close connection between Scripture and the Spirit suggests that the authority of Scripture is ultimately derived from the authority of the Spirit who speaks in and through the text. The same Spirit who forms the Christian community also guides that community in the production of the biblical texts. Viewed from a historical perspective, the texts of Scripture and the notion of the Bible as a whole are the products of the communities of faith that produced them. The compilation of Scripture occurred within the context of the faith community, and the biblical documents represent the self-understanding of the communities in which they were developed. Indeed, one of the most significant but often overlooked elements of the texts of Scripture is that they reflect the life of the communities that produced them and the ways in which these ancient peoples understood how God was present among them.

Frequently, the earliest communities of faith experienced God in unexpected ways that strained their ability to follow and cope. In the New Testament, think of the book of Acts and the new challenges that constantly confront the followers of Jesus as they try to relate their understanding of the law to the work of the Spirit—Peter and dietary laws, the relationship to the gentiles, and the question of circumcision at the Jerusalem Council. This dynamic continues into the present as communities wrestle with new questions that arise in the proclamation of the good news.

What unifies this relationship between Scripture and the proclamation of the church is the work of the Spirit. The illuminating work of the Spirit brought forth these writings from the context of the community in accordance with the witness of that community. This work of illumination has not ceased with the adoption of the canon. Rather, it continues as the Spirit attunes the contemporary community of faith to understand Scripture and apply it afresh to its own context in accordance with the mission of God in the world.

The contemporary process of illumination parallels that experienced by the ancient faith communities. For instance, the prophets offer sharp critique and condemnation of certain attitudes and practices within their ancient faith communities. This dynamic continues in the present as elements of the tradition of the church continue to be wrestled with, and sometimes deemed inappropriate, to the trajectories of the gospel and the deepest intentions of the faith community. Scripture, tradition, and proclamation are the effects of working out the ongoing meaning of divine revelation by the Christian community. This working out is characterized by a remarkable pluralism in both the witness of Scripture and the proclamation of the church.

In the multifaceted and diverse collection of writings that make up canonical Scripture, we find a diversity of literary forms—such as narrative, law, prophecy, wisdom, parable, epistle, and others. And within each of these forms, we have the expression of numerous perspectives. This is reflected in diverse law codes, chronologies, ethical and theological assertions, as well as four Gospel accounts. Indeed, the presence of Matthew, Mark, Luke, and John in the canon, each with its distinctive perspective on the life and ministry of Jesus, alerts us to the pluriform character of the gospel itself.

Attempts to cover over these diverse perspectives through the imposition of a single conception of the diverse whole not only miss the diversity that is woven into the very fabric of Scripture, but also fail to perceive the divine intention of God for the world. Pluralism is an essential component of God's universal design and purposes for creation. One of the implications of this is that a single description of the Christian faith can never be adequate and sufficient for all times and places. The multiplicity of the biblical witness stands against such a notion. Christian faith is, by its very nature, pluralist. That is to say, it is according to the witness of the whole community rather than only a part.

Further, the multiplicity of biblical texts is not incidental to the shape of the community from which they emerged or that which is envisioned in the community's future. Attempts to suppress the plurality of the biblical witness by means of an overarching, universalistic account lead to serious distortions of the gospel and the community that is called to bear witness to it. The plurality of forms and perspectives embedded in Scripture reminds us that no single voice, community, or interpretive approach will be adequate to convey the revelation and purposes of God.

With respect to the proclamation of the church, this pluralism is anticipated in the opening of Acts. Following the resurrection, Jesus's disciples asked him, "Lord, is this the time when you will restore the kingdom to Israel?" In response, he replied, "You will receive power when the Holy Spirit has come upon you; and you will be my witnesses in Jerusalem, in all Judea and Samaria, and to the ends of the earth" (Acts 1:6, 8). After speaking these words to his chosen apostles, Jesus was lifted up and taken from their sight. The apostles returned to Jerusalem to wait and pray. On the day of Pentecost, a strong wind came upon them and they were filled with the Holy Spirit and began to speak in other languages (2:1–4). The text goes on to say that a large and diverse gathering who were present for this phenomenon were bewildered because they each heard their own language being spoken. Those who experienced this linguistic phenomenon were reportedly amazed and perplexed, asking one another what it meant (2:5–12).

The meaning of this Pentecostal plurality is significant for understanding the mission of God and the calling of the church to bear witness to the ends of the earth. The action of the Spirit here effectively decenters any particular language or culture with respect to the proclamation of the gospel. The implication is that no single language or culture is to be viewed as the prime or inseparable conduit of the gospel message. Christians have sought to make the Bible available to people in different cultures by translating it into their languages, rather than insisting that new followers learn the biblical languages. This principle has been a key component in the development of Christian approaches to mission shaped around the notion of plurality and contextuality.[1]

This has led to the translation of the Bible into nearly 2,400 different vernacular languages and the establishment of a culturally and socially diverse witnessing community throughout the world. This new community is called to live out an alternative way of life in the world as every tribe and nation bears witness to the good news of God's love for all people. In keeping with the calling of the Christian community to bear witness to the ends of the earth, the church in the aftermath of Pentecost emerged as a multifaceted and multidirectional movement. This points to the infinite translatability of the gospel as it encounters new cultures and social contexts.[2]

Such translatability continually results in fresh adaptations of the Christian faith as the message of the gospel spreads across national, tribal, linguistic, and ethnic boundaries, engaging culture after culture, social setting after

1. On this approach to mission, see Sanneh, *Translating the Message.*

2. On the notion of infinite translatability, see Bevans and Schroeder, *Constants in Context.*

social setting, and situation after situation. In the task of participating in the purposes of God, the church continually reinvents itself to meet the challenges of relating the gospel to new peoples and new cultures. In this activity, the experience and understanding of what it means to be the church arises from the ongoing engagement of the gospel with culture.

This results in an irreducible plurality that characterizes the witness of the Christian community. The very nature of the call to proclaim the good news of the love of God to the ends of the earth and embody it among all peoples and situations for the good of the world leads inevitably to diversity and multiplicity.

Viewed in this light, we see that plurality rather than uniformity characterizes the story of Christianity. Pentecost is indicative of the Spirit's work and paradigmatic for the spreading of the gospel message. From this perspective, the diversity of the Christian faith is *not*, as some approaches to church and theology might seem to suggest, a problem that needs to be overcome. Instead, this plurality is part of the divine design and intention for the church as the image of God, body of Christ, and dwelling place of the Spirit in the world. Christian plurality is a good thing, not something that needs to be struggled against, overturned, or corrected.[3]

From this perspective, we can say that as the word of God and *normative* witness to revelation, Scripture consists of inspired human speech-acts that bear authentic witness to the divine speech-acts of revelation. As the word of God and *paradigmatic* human witness to revelation, Scripture also invites an even greater plurality than that contained in its pages in order that the witness of the church to the purposes of God may be continually expanded to all people.

Christian Pluralism

We've suggested that a proper understanding of revelation and Scripture leads to the conclusion that Christian faith is pluralist by its very nature.[4] The fullness of this plurality in revelation, Scripture, and the tradition of the church points beyond the mere acknowledgment that the Christian faith is characterized by diversity and difference—a position that can be

3. On the notion of the church as the image of God, body of Christ, and dwelling place of the Spirit, see Franke, *Missional Theology*, 41–56.

4. For a more detailed discussion of the plurality of Christian faith and truth itself, see Franke, *Manifold Witness*.

called Christian pluralism. While we use the terms plurality and pluralism somewhat interchangeably in this volume, they can be understood as having slightly different connotations. While the idea of Christian plurality may simply be construed as an awareness of the diversity of the tradition, Christian pluralism takes a more philosophical position, suggesting that pluralism is normative for Christian faith. For us, Christian plurality, as we have described it, points to the idea of Christian pluralism as a hermeneutical, theological, and philosophical position. What are the implications of this Christian pluralism for the witness of the church? We will briefly mention four.

First, Christian pluralism reminds us of the contextuality and inexhaustible fullness of the gospel. This is made manifest in the cultural expansion of the church as communities emerge and interact with one another. The process of translation and contextualization is not something that takes place after the biblical texts, their interpretations, and corresponding doctrines are established. Rather, it is fully present in all of these forms of witness and cannot be removed or eliminated. Contextuality is an inherent part of the process of understanding and communication.

From this perspective, biblical interpretation and communication are always matters involving the recontextualization of texts in a variety of social and historical settings. This ongoing activity of recontextualization in and for a diversity of cultural settings is the essence of Christian witness from the perspective of pluralism.

Second, Christian pluralism is inherently intercultural. This interculturality involves understanding the social contexts of other interpreters as well as texts, which significantly reconfigures common notions of Christian witness with respect to the communication of the gospel. This is particularly true with respect to traditional forms of cross-cultural activity in which the recipients of the gospel message are treated as the objects for conversion. They are expected to receive the message as presented if they are to benefit from its promises. Such an approach leads to colonization, a situation in which the message functions like the introduction of an alien ideology that, if accepted, undermines and subverts the ecosystem of the existing culture with detrimental effects on its participants.

Instead, the model of Christian pluralism invites intercultural understanding and involves genuine and loving concern for others *and* the cultural settings that shape their identity. With respect to Christian witness, living out and proclaiming the good news of the gospel becomes an enterprise in mutual understanding in which all of the participants provide crucial and necessary elements to the discourse.

Third, Christian pluralism is dialogical. It reminds us that while the world needs the gospel, the church needs to listen to the world in order to understand the gospel more fully. Justo González conceives of the mission of the church as being shaped not only by the need of the world to hear the gospel, but also by the need of the church to hear and listen to the world in all the diversity of its nations, cultures, and ethnicities.[5] In this way the church will have a fuller understanding of the gospel as people from all the earth bring the richness of their experience to bear on its proclamation.

This dialogical interaction is vital to the witness of an appropriately pluralist church and provides a necessary resistance to both an inflexible dogmatism that restricts the truth and fullness of the gospel and an "anything goes" relativism that eclipses it. Listening with empathy to the experiences and perspectives of people from differing cultural contexts and situations helps Christian communities to resist the danger of allowing the gospel message to be either overly accommodated to culture or viewed as something entirely apart from culture.

Fourth, Christian pluralism reminds us that while cultural, ethnic, ideological, and religious diversity and plurality are given facts of life on earth, genuine pluralism is not. Pluralism is rather an achievement waiting to be realized in the face of the enmity and hostility that exists among the peoples of the earth. In response to this situation, God has sent Jesus to reconcile human beings not only to God, but also to each other, for the sake of peace. The church is called to bear witness to, and participate in, this salvific work of peace-making pluralism by becoming a new and inclusive community made up of all the peoples of the earth. Indeed, the Spirit is given to the church for this very purpose.

This divine plan is ultimately intended to restore harmony to creation and bring peace to the earth. Participation in this pluralism doesn't mean giving up Christian commitments. Far from it. It means leaning into them more fully. As Lamin Sanneh concludes, "For most of us it is difficult enough to respect those with whom we might disagree, to say nothing of those who might be different from us in culture, language, and tradition. For all of us pluralism can be a rock of stumbling, but for God it is the cornerstone of the universal design."[6] Pluralism is God's intention for the

5. González, *Out of Every Tribe and Nation*, 28–29.
6. Sanneh, *Translating the Message*, 27.

world, the cornerstone of the universal design. *Christian* pluralism is the particular calling of the Christian community to embrace and participate in this larger divine design by loving God and our neighbors more faithfully for the sake of the world that God loves.

The Spirit, the Scriptures, and the Church

The Christian tradition has always been concerned to bind word and Spirit together as a means of providing the conceptual framework for interpretation. We suggest that ultimate authority in the church is the Spirit speaking in and through the texts of Scripture. This means that Christian belief and practice cannot be determined merely by appeal to biblical exegesis alone or to any supposed word from the Spirit that effectively disregards such exegesis. The reading and interpretation of the text are for the purpose of listening to the voice of the Spirit who speaks in and through Scripture to the church in the present. This means that the Bible is authoritative in that it is the vehicle through which the Spirit speaks.

Through Scripture, the Spirit continually instructs the church as the historically extended community of Christ's followers in the midst of the opportunities and challenges of life in the contemporary world. In effect, the Spirit appropriates the biblical text for the purpose of speaking to us today. This appropriation does not come independently of the so-called original meaning of the text. Indeed, careful historical exegesis is a crucial component in attempting to understand the meaning of Scripture. The speaking of the Spirit, however, is not bound up solely with the supposed original intent of the authors and editors of the biblical texts. Contemporary proponents of textual intentionality, such as Paul Ricœur, explain that although an author creates a literary text, it takes on a life of its own once it has been written. While the ways in which the text is structured shape the meanings the reader discerns in the text, the author's intentions come to be distanced from the meanings of the work. In this sense, a text can be viewed metaphorically as having its own intention. This textual intention has its genesis in the author's intention but is not equated with or exhausted by it.

Therefore, we must not conclude that exegesis alone can exhaust the Spirit's speaking to us through the text. While the Spirit appropriates the text in its internal meaning, the goal of this appropriation is to guide the church in the variegated circumstances of particular contemporary settings. Hence, we realize that the Spirit's speaking does not come through the text in isolation but rather in the context of specific historical-cultural situations and as part of an extended interpretive tradition.

The assertion that the Spirit appropriates the text of Scripture and speaks in and through it to those in contemporary settings leads to the question of the goal or effect of the Spirit's speaking. What does the Spirit seek to accomplish in the act of speaking through the text of Scripture?

We suggest that through the process of addressing readers in various contemporary settings, the Spirit creates a world. Sociologists point out that religion plays a significant role in world construction through a set of beliefs and practices that provide a particular way of looking at reality. From this perspective, the biblical documents point beyond themselves to meanings that may be described as being "in front of" texts rather than "behind" them. Texts project a way of being in the world, a mode of existence, a pattern of life, and point toward a possible world. The Bible stands in a central position relative to the practice of the Christian community. The community reads Scripture as the primary lens through which it views the narrative world it inhabits. In short, the text calls a new world into being.

This capacity for world construction, while bound closely to the text, does not lie in the text itself. Instead, the construction of such a world is ultimately the work of the Spirit, speaking in and through the biblical texts to human communities as the instrumentality of world creation. The world co-created by the Spirit and the communities that are addressed is neither the world surrounding the ancient text nor the contemporary world, but rather the eschatological world God intends for creation as disclosed, displayed, and anticipated by Scripture. The ongoing work of the Spirit is manifest in the appropriation of the biblical narrative in order to speak to the church for the purpose of creating a socially constructed world that finds its coherence in Jesus Christ in accordance with, and in anticipation of, the real world as it is willed by God.

As Scripture makes clear, the world as God wills it to be is not a present reality, but rather lies in the eschatological future. Thus, while acknowledging that there is indeed a certain objective reality to the world, it is important to recognize that this objectivity is not that of a static reality existing outside of, and co-temporally with, our socially and linguistically constructed realities. That reality is not what some might call the world as it is. Instead, the biblical narratives set forth the objectivity of the world as God wills it. Hence, Jesus taught his disciples to pray, "Your will be done on earth as it is in heaven" (Matt 6:10). Again, biblically speaking, the most real world is the future, eschatological world that God will establish in the new creation. Because this future reality, described in Scripture as the reign of God, cannot be shaken (Heb 12:26–28), it is far more real, objective, and actual than the present world, which is even now passing away (1 Cor 7:31). In this way, the biblical narratives point to what might be called eschatological realism.

Connecting this eschatological realism to the insights of social constructionists,[7] we note that human beings, as bearers of the divine image, are called to participate in God's work of constructing a world in the present that reflects God's own eschatological will for creation. This call has a strongly linguistic dimension due to the role of language in the task of world-construction. Through the constructive power of language, the Christian community anticipates the divine eschatological world that stands at the climax of the biblical narrative in which all creation finds its connectedness in Jesus Christ (Col 1:17), who is the Word (John 1:1) and the ordering principle of the cosmos.

Hence, Christian participation in the purposes of God may be construed as Christocentric in its communitarian focus and Christotelic in its eschatological orientation. The eschatological future is anticipated in the present through the work of the Spirit, who leads the church into truth (1 John 2:27). From this perspective, the Christian community bears witness to the truth of the gospel through the construction and proclamation of a social linguistic world that finds its coherence in Jesus Christ in accordance with the will of God. As such, the church is called to be a provisional demonstration of God's will for all creation. Through the inspiration of Scripture, the Spirit forms witnessing communities that participate in the purposes of God by embodying God's love in the way of Jesus Christ for the sake of the world.

It seems to us that the threefold form of the word of God described here effectively removes the word of God from human control—which, of course, we never have—without denying human involvement in any of its three forms. It is the event of the word of God that liberates us from the tyranny of

7. The thesis of social constructionism is that, rather than inhabiting a world of meaning that exists apart from human interaction and engagement, human beings actually create meaning through the language, rituals, and symbols we construct. In other words, we live in a linguistically construed social-cultural world of our own creation. For a classic discussion of the significance of social constructionism for religion, see Berger, *Sacred Canopy*. On the implications of social constructionism for theology, see Franke, *Character of Theology*.

philosophies, ideologies, and traditions of interpretation that imprison our imaginations to the detriment of the human community.

Jesus deconstructs prior assumptions and practices—such as those found in Deut 20—when he exhorts his audience to "love [their] enemies and pray for those who persecute [them]" (Matt 5:44). In saying this, Jesus is inviting a radical openness to the "other," reminding us that God's economy is not of this world. He affirms the freedom of the word of God in the face of the traditions of reflection that have formed around that word. Even our allegiance to the Bible can draw us away from God's purposes if and when we read it in a static and absolutist fashion, leaving Scripture and ourselves shackled. As the exodus from Egyptian bondage—Israel's primal story—illustrates, and as Jesus himself repeatedly demonstrates, God is a God of liberation. Thus, the word of God—if, in fact, it is God's word—must be a liberating word. Scripture is an instrument in that liberative process, not its end.

CHAPTER 6

Missional Hermeneutics and Theological Interpretation

ONE OF THE THEMES throughout this volume has been the idea that God has purposes in the world. God is engaged, not neutral. In Scripture, we see a record of people wrestling to discern those purposes, believing that God has made them known through the action of divine self-disclosure. Examples include the direct speech of God, the actions that accompany and correspond to the words of God, the divine explanation of God's particular actions, and for Christians, the life and teaching of Jesus. Testimony to these actions in written form is a means of bearing witness to them and passing them on for future generations. Within the canon itself, we encounter attempts to interpret these actions theologically. That is, biblical writers were themselves attempting to discern larger patterns within the particular actions and texts. Sometimes we even encounter the reframing of the texts themselves in order to articulate those patterns and display them in support of a particular understanding of divine purposes. Perhaps the most illustrative example of this is found in the writings of Paul, as he attempts to perceive the larger purposes of God in the texts of what Christians have come to call the Old Testament—though this kind of reinterpretation and reframing was already evident within and among Old Testament texts themselves, long before Paul. This is an example of the sort of theological interpretation that has continued throughout the history of the church as interpreters have sought to identify and understand the purposes of God in the world.

Missional hermeneutics is a particular approach to theological interpretation that places emphasis on discerning the larger purposes of God displayed in and through the texts of Scripture. As we have already discussed, the Spirit plays an active role in this ongoing process of interpretation.

In the act of speaking in and through the texts of Scripture, the Spirit creates communities that seek to participate in the purposes of God. Thus we read the various texts in the light of the whole of the biblical message, mediated through the teaching of Jesus, listening for the Spirit's voice guiding us as we become the Spirit-constructed missional community of faith in the contemporary context in which we are situated. In what follows, we suggest that reading theologically means reading for the Spirit, reading as "other," reading the patterns, and reading in community.

Reading the Bible Theologically

The beginning point for theological interpretation of Scripture is the presupposition that the Bible is the vehicle through which the Spirit speaks to us, and the primary means by which the Spirit forms individuals and communities for participation in God's purposes. This notion is rooted in the Johannine assertion that the Spirit is sent to lead us into truth by reminding the followers of Jesus of his teaching: that "the Advocate, the Holy Spirit, whom the Father will send in my name, will teach you everything and remind you of all that I have said to you" (John 14:26).

This Christocentric tradition finds its roots in the early church and is something that we take to be a central focus of missional hermeneutics. Through Scripture the Spirit lays hold of the lives of readers and communities, calling them into a life of service connected to the mission of Jesus. In this way, spiritual formation is always a major goal of biblical interpretation. Missional biblical interpretation seeks to bring together diligent and sustained hermeneutical reflection and patience in listening for the Spirit's voice speaking through it. Readers come to the text with both open hearts and searching minds, diligently seeking to discern the purposes of God. This is because the intentions of the Spirit speaking in and through the texts is accessible to those who are in experiential and participatory contact with the missional realities to which the text bears witness.

Reading for the Spirit entails listening to what the Spirit is saying through the text (exegesis) to us in our context (hermeneutics). Coming to Scripture seeking to hear the Spirit's voice thus requires that we distinguish between exegesis and hermeneutics. Ultimately, though, exegesis and hermeneutics are fused together in a creative synthesis that brings together the results and conclusions of historical investigation and the situation in life of contemporary interpreters.

Because we are always located as readers, theological readings of the text always move from and return to the contemporary situation in which the faith community is living, even though this hermeneutical process involves the use of exegetical methods. We read Scripture so that the Spirit might nurture us in the ongoing process of living as the contemporary embodiment of the paradigmatic narratives of Scripture. Reading Scripture theologically entails reading the Bible as a whole, confident that the Spirit speaks through the texts to create the eschatological world according to the ultimate intentions and purposes of God.

Reading the text to hear the voice of the Spirit leads to a second element of what it means to read theologically. We approach the text conscious that we come to it as "other" to "other." Fernando Segovia summarizes what it means to view both the text and the reader as "other." He writes, "Rather than positing any type of direct or immediate entrance into the text, the hermeneutic of otherness and engagement argues for the distantiation from the text as a working desideratum, emphasizing thereby the historical and cultural remoteness of the text."[1] This approach views the reader as a socially and culturally conditioned "other" both to the text itself and to other readers. Consequently, a strict objectivity arising from a presumption to universality must give way to "a self-conscious exposition and analysis of the reader's strategy for reading, the theoretical foundations behind this strategy, and the social location underlying such a strategy."[2] As Segovia indicates, theological reading requires that we acknowledge the integrity of the text within its own world, even though that world might appear strange to us. It means as well that we acknowledge the distance that stands between our world and the world of the text. This is what we intend when we say that we must seek to read the text in ways that are responsible and attentive to its own forms of communicating, acknowledging the particularity of our own social location and its distance, or otherness, from that of the text.

1. Segovia, "Text as Other," 294.
2. Segovia, "Text as Other," 295.

Acknowledging this twofold distance leads to the realization that the goal of our theological reading is not to alter the text to fit our world. Indeed, attempting to do so would simply undermine the integrity of the text. Nor should our intent be to alter ourselves to fit into the world of the text—as if this were even possible. The hermeneutical process we are describing does not transform the world of the reader into an earlier historical reality, such as the biblical world, through which we might think that we have access through the text. Reading the text as "other" to "other" entails maintaining the integrity of the text while acknowledging that it is embedded in what to the contemporary reader is a strange and largely foreign world.

At the same time, contemporary readers expect that through this reading the Spirit will fashion a new world in their present. And this new world that the Spirit calls readers to inhabit is none other than the eschatological world of God's design. In short, to read the text theologically—as "other" to "other"—is to invite the Spirit to engage in divine work in the lives of the readers through the text, which is the Spirit's instrumentality. That we always come to Scripture as "other" reminds us that we are always "at a distance" from the intentions of the writers of Scripture. We read as those engaged with the strange, new world of the Bible and as such, we cannot posit a simple one-to-one connection between the world of the biblical text and our contemporary situation. Through the mediation of the Spirit, however, we believe that we are able to discern the deepest intentions of the gospel in our particular social locations.

A third element of reading theologically consists of discerning the deeper patterns of convergence that emerge throughout the witness of the biblical texts. We read the individual texts of Scripture in light of the whole, again seeking to get at the deepest intentions of the biblical narratives, while understanding that our perspectives about the whole are informed by our reading of the individual texts. This suggests that we read the Bible theologically as we read with the goal of seeing patterns of convergence in Scripture. Here, we must be careful to avoid the common practice of prooftexting in the task of theological construction. Appealing to individual texts in reaching theological conclusions is, of course, crucial. Prooftexting errs, however, by simply selecting particular verses in support of a particular theological system. Any conclusions are already foreordained. In the process, prooftexting ends up treating the Bible simplistically, turning it into a collection of theological resources rather than a set of diverse texts to be read theologically. Reading the Bible theologically provides a corrective to this approach.

Theological reading views Scripture not as a storehouse of facts waiting to systematized, but as a testimony to the ongoing work of God with humankind, a work that climaxes with the Spirit calling into being the eschatological community intended by God in the act of creation. Consequently, we read scriptural texts theologically as we seek converging patterns present throughout the documents. This theological reading involves looking for the ways in which different parts come together as a whole. Most particularly, we read the texts in light of their convergence in an interpretive outlook that finds its coherence in the mission of God ultimately made known in Jesus Christ.

The task of recognizing patterns requires that interpretative conclusions are drawn from the full range of diverse biblical texts. Reading theologically also invites us to the conclusion that canonical Scripture is a collection of polyphonic writings with thematic unity. We view the various and distinctive books as finding coherence in the ultimate purposes of God revealed in Jesus. This coherence does not ultimately rest with the inherent singularity of voice the texts themselves supposedly display. Nor is it dependent on any supposed singularity of the church's decision as to which books are canonical (for in fact the church has never been in complete agreement on this point). Rather, the singularity of voice we claim for Scripture is ultimately the singularity of the Spirit who speaks in and through the texts. Reading the Bible theologically means approaching the texts as embodying a unity of basic purpose. This unity of purpose brings the Old and New Testaments together as comprising one canon.

Reading the Bible as one canon forms the basis for reading the texts of the Hebrew Bible as Christian Scripture. The unitary purpose of the Bible as a whole leads to the realization that the material realities given in the Hebrew Bible are not merely shadows of spiritual realities more fully and accurately described in the New Testament. Rather, they are also promises of a spiritual reality given first to ancient Israel and later to Christians. As this approach to Christian Scripture in two Testaments indicates, theology assists the reading of the Bible. It alerts the reader to read within the context of the unitive patterns that bring the texts into a canonical whole. Those who approach the biblical text from the perspective of missional hermeneutics propose that the mission of God provides this thematic unity and canonical unity. They recognize that the message of Jesus as being in deep continuity with the Hebrew Bible, such that it constitutes a critical mistake to pit the teaching and mission of Jesus against that which we find in the Old Testament. The teaching of Jesus as depicted in the Gospels constitutes an ongoing continuation of the vision for the repair of the world and its ultimate destiny as a community where everyone has enough and no one needs to be afraid.

A final element of reading theologically involves reading in community. We have noted repeatedly that the Spirit speaks through the biblical text so as to fashion communities that live the paradigmatic missional biblical narrative in contemporary contexts. The goal of our reading the text, therefore, is to hear the Spirit's voice forming us into such communities. This understanding leads to the conclusion that reading the text theologically entails reading within community. This also reminds us that our readings of Scripture always occur in the midst of others.

Reading within community occurs as we approach the text conscious that we are participants in faith communities that span the ages and the globe. This consciousness involves recognizing the theological tradition within which we stand as contemporary readers of the text. Because we come to the text as participants in a trajectory of faith, who seek to understand the whole of Scripture as the work of the Spirit's speaking to us, it is important to grow in our awareness of the history of interpretation. An awareness of the theological traditions of the church, historically and globally, can assist us in this process. Understanding that our communal reading occurs in the midst of an ongoing conversation about reading the texts faithfully, we are invited to look beyond ourselves and our own conclusions in the interpretation of Scripture. The process of reading the Bible faithfully is enhanced as we take seriously the attempts of those who have gone before us to engage in the hermeneutical task that now occupies us, namely, that of listening to the Spirit speaking through the biblical texts.

Reading within community occurs as well as we approach the text conscious that we are participants in contemporary communities. This consciousness entails the desire to take seriously the attempts of others to understand what the Spirit is saying to the faith community. Such attempts are both local and global. Hence, we do well to consider the manifold voices of faith communities in various settings around the world as they seek to discern how the Spirit is guiding them through Scripture in the task of being Christ's disciples in their local contexts.

Being conscious that we are participants in the contemporary Christian community means reading the text within the local congregational setting. We come to Scripture aware that we are participants in a concrete, visible fellowship of disciples in covenant with each other. In the end, our goal is to hear what the Spirit is saying to this particular congregation and to these particular believers who share together the mandate of being a fellowship of believers in this specific setting. Obviously, this involves engaging in the hermeneutical task within the gathered community. But sensitivity to reading within community extends to our individual interpretive efforts—requiring awareness that while we read in the company of the larger global church, we are also participants in a particular local community. It is in our participation in the local community that we are most deeply formed and transformed for participation in the mission of God.

It should be clear from this conception of reading the Bible theologically that we are speaking more of faithful postures rather than particular interpretative positions. Missional hermeneutics respects the history of biblical interpretation and theology, while at the same time resisting the temptation to absolutize any particular interpretive conclusions as decisive for all places and times. Such absolutes have too often worked against the purposes of God and led to the oppression and marginalization of those who do not agree with or acknowledge the established conclusions of those in power. In addition, absolute and definitively certain interpretative and theological conclusions work against the freedom of God and plurality of the word of God discussed earlier. In the words of Karl Barth, we must always begin again at the beginning so that our hermeneutical efforts will not unintentionally belie the very reality to which we seek to bear witness. We conclude the chapter with three interpretative postures that characterize the kind of missional hermeneutics that we have in mind.

Theological Postures of Missional Hermeneutics

We have discussed the primacy of love in the Christian tradition, and it is this reality that gives rise to the posture of missional hermeneutics. We might simply speak of this as the posture of love, but here we suggest some additional specificity. The love that characterizes the mission of God from all eternity shapes the mission of God in the world. The centrality of love and relationality in the human expression of God's love in and for the world leads to a hermeneutical posture of openness and commitment to the other. In this conception, meaning is not a static entity that can be casually grasped and assimilated by human beings. Rather, meaning making is relational and participatory. We do not know meaning apart from the relations it engenders with God, other human beings, and the created order. From this perspective, interpretation and the work of meaning making is not something done in a once-for-all fashion. It cannot be reified as though it were a commodity that can be easily accessed and controlled by human beings, with the constant danger that it will then be put to use in ways that empower its holders at the expense of others.

Instead, the work of hermeneutics is an ongoing task that requires the commitment of our entire being to the love of God revealed in Jesus Christ through the power of the Spirit. It is a reality that constantly calls on us to privilege others above ourselves in accordance with the teaching and example of Jesus, "who, though he existed in the form of God, did not regard equality with God as something to be grasped, but emptied himself, taking the form of a slave, assuming human likeness. And being found in appearance as a human, he humbled himself and became obedient to the point of death—even death on a cross" (Phil 2:6–8). Based on the example of Jesus, Paul exhorts his readers, "Do nothing from selfish ambition or empty conceit, but in humility regard others as better than yourselves. Let each of you look not to your own interests but to the interests of others" (Phil 2:3).

In the Christian tradition, we are invited to see Jesus in the faces of others, particularly the poor and marginalized, and also to see God in Jesus. In this context, Jesus becomes the focal point for a theological orientation toward the other. Among the connotations associated with the idea of otherness are philosophical, ethical, and eschatological concerns. In the broadest terms, the "other" is viewed as anything or anyone that falls outside of one's own categories. Here the realm and context of a person's own particular self is constantly confronted and pierced by that which is "other," that which cannot be confined in the categories of sameness.

The challenge with respect to this aspect of otherness is to refrain from its violation by reducing it to the self-enclosed realm of the same and thereby forcing it into a homogenous, self-made mold that serves to efface it and eliminate its distinctive difference, its very otherness in relation to the same. Recognizing this challenge has significance for the knowledge of God made known in the face of the other—which cannot be merely summarized, conceptualized, or possessed. Instead, in the face of the other, in the very difference and strangeness of the other, the ultimate irreducibility of the other to sameness, we glimpse something of the epiphany of transcendence. Connected with openness to being nurtured by the other is the concept of hybridity, which represents the persistence of difference in unity. This is not the same as syncretism, which entails the attempt to unite opposing principles. Hybridity stands for resistance to hardened differences based on binary oppositions and the refusal to absorb all difference into a hegemonic notion of sameness.

Some will also recognize this line of thought as consonant with postmodern theory. At its core, postmodernity is a movement that resists the totalizing power of reason in order to celebrate difference and diversity—a commitment that, as we understand them, both theology and missional hermeneutics share. The agenda of openness to the other leads to a commitment to plurality consistent with the revelation of the word of God. This is what accounts for the wide array of disparate discourses that share a commitment to postmodern thought. Reformed theologian James Olthuis summarizes this commitment admirably:

> Ethically, postmodern discourses share an alertness to plurality
> and a vigilance on behalf of the other. Modernist rational ethics,
> in its Enlightenment dream of a world increasingly controlled by
> a pure rationality, has shown itself not only blind and indifferent
> to those who are other and different, those who fall outside the
> dominant discourse, but violent and oppressive to them.[3]

Following the concerns of postmodern thought at this point, the kind of missional hermeneutics we envision and propose invites resistance to the totalizing structures of interpretation in order to celebrate difference and diversity as a means of remaining open and committed to the witness of others. We suggest that hermeneutical postures shaped by the mission of God will continually be characterized by openness and commitment to voices of others in the task of Christian witness.

God's love does not seek to assimilate the "other." We suggest that the emphasis on otherness in the life of the triune God, extended into the world through the revelation of God in Jesus Christ, can and should shape our hermeneutical assumptions and intuitions. If we are to resist the dangers of our own inherent cultural accommodation, we must become and remain open to the witness of others. One of the ways in which openness and commitment to the voices of others bears on interpretative practice is found in contexts where the dominance of a particular set of social and cultural assumptions

3. Olthuis, "Face-to-Face," 135.

and presuppositions have served to stamp the Bible in its particular cultural image. When this occurs, the voices of those who do not participate in the assumptions and presuppositions of the majority are marginalized or eclipsed, often under the guise of claims that they are not being faithful to Scripture or the Christian tradition by seeking to import a particular cultural agenda into the interpretation of Scripture.

Openness to plurality and difference calls on us to recognize the limitations of our own perspectives and experiences and invites a life lived for the sake of others as the means by which we can be delivered from the prison of our own imaginations and begin to experience something of the reality made known by God in Jesus Christ. The posture of openness and commitment to the other and the corresponding commitment to plurality for the sake faithful Christian witness are vital for missional hermeneutics as we understand it.

In keeping with its commitment to otherness, contextuality, and plurality, we suggest that missional hermeneutics needs to offer and maintain a postfoundational philosophical posture. As we have noted, classic or strong foundationalism has led some contemporary interpreters to shackle Scripture with modern philosophical positions that are alien to the contexts in which the texts were written and in conflict with its deepest intentions. The Enlightenment quest for epistemological certitude deeply shaped the modern era through the rejection of premodern notions of authority, replacing them with the notion of indubitable beliefs that are accessible to all individuals.

Philosophically, foundationalism is a theory concerned with the justification of knowledge. It maintains that beliefs must be justified by their relationship to other beliefs and that the chain of justifications that results from this procedure must not be circular or endless, but must have a terminus in foundational beliefs that are immune from criticism and cannot be called into question. The goal to be attained through the identification of indubitable foundations is a universal knowledge that transcends time and context. In keeping with this pursuit, the ideals of human knowledge since the Enlightenment have tended to focus on the universal, the general, and the theoretical rather than on the local, the particular, and the practical.

This conception of knowledge came to dominate most of biblical interpretation and theology, and conceptions of the Bible and Christian faith were developed in accordance with its dictates. In the nineteenth and twentieth centuries, the foundationalist impulse produced a theological and hermeneutical division between the left and the right. Liberals constructed theology upon the foundation of an unassailable religious experience, while conservatives looked to an error-free Bible as the incontrovertible foundation of their theology. It is interesting to note that, for all their differences, both groups were drawing from commonly held foundationalist conceptions of knowledge. In other words, liberal and conservative theologians can often be viewed as working out theological details from two different sides of the same modernist, foundationalist coin.

Postmodern hermeneutics raises two related but distinct questions for the modern foundationalist enterprise. First, is such an approach to knowledge *possible*? And second, is it *desirable*? These questions are connected with what may be viewed as the two major branches of postmodern hermeneutical philosophy: the hermeneutics of finitude and the hermeneutics of suspicion. The challenges to foundationalism are not only philosophical, however, but also emerge from the context of Christian theology. Merold Westphal suggests that postmodern theory, with respect to hermeneutical philosophy, may be properly appropriated for the task of explicitly Christian thought on theological grounds: "The hermeneutics of finitude is a meditation on the meaning of human createdness, and the hermeneutics of suspicion is a meditation on the meaning of human fallenness."[4] From our perspective, the questions raised by postmodern hermeneutics are consistent with the posture of missional thought with respect to the possibility and desirability of foundationalism. Indeed, they both lead to similar conclusions.

First, modern foundationalism is an impossible dream for finite human beings whose outlooks are always limited and shaped by the particular contexts from which they emerge. And second, the modern foundationalist emphasis on the inherent goodness of knowledge is shattered by the sinfulness of human beings who desire to seize control of the epistemic process in order to empower themselves and further their own ends, often at the expense of others. The limitations of finitude and the flawed condition of human nature mean that epistemic foundationalism is neither possible nor desirable for created and sinful persons. This double critique of foundationalism, emerging as it does from the perspectives of both postmodern philosophy and Christian thought, suggests to us the appropriateness and suitability, given the current intellectual situation, of a postfoundationalist (or nonfoundationalist) posture for missional hermeneutics.

4. Westphal, *Overcoming Onto-theology*, xx.

One of the most significant elements of postfoundationalism for missional hermeneutics is its inherent commitment to contextuality that requires the opening of theological conversation to the voices of persons and communities who have often been excluded from the traditional discourses of Western thought. The adoption of a postfoundational philosophical posture in the practice of missional hermeneutics thus leads to the conclusion that no single human perspective, whether of an individual, a particular community, or a theological tradition, is adequate to do full justice to the truth of God's revelation in Christ. Evangelical theologian Richard Mouw points to this issue as one of his own motivations for reflecting seriously on postmodern themes:

> As many Christians from other parts of the world challenge our "North Atlantic" theologies, they too ask us to think critically about our own cultural location, as well as about how we have sometimes blurred the boundaries between what is essential to the Christian message and the doctrine and frameworks we have borrowed from various Western philosophical traditions.[5]

Adoption of a postfoundationalist posture requires that missional hermeneutics manifest a critical awareness of the role of culture and social location in the process of biblical and theological interpretation.

Again, a postfoundational approach to hermeneutics places emphasis on the local, the particular, and the practical, rather than on the universal, the general, and the theoretical. Such a posture is committed to setting aside any and all appeals to presumed self-evident, non-inferential, or incorrigible grounds for interpretive claims. Postfoundationalism rejects the notion that among the many procedures and methods that make up an approach to the reading and interpretation of texts there must be irrefutable approaches that are immune to criticism and provide the certain basis upon which all other conclusions and methods are based. In our vision of missional hermeneutics, all conclusions are open to criticism and reconstruction, including those in this volume.

This does not mean, as is sometimes alleged, that those adopting a postfoundational hermeneutical posture cannot make assertions or maintain strong convictions that may be vigorously defended. To take this posture is not to eschew the possibility of conviction. Rather, it is to accept the inescapable reality that interpretation is, by nature, a self-correcting enterprise that critically examines all claims, construals, constructions, and

5. Mouw, "Delete the 'Post,'" 22.

background theories. Such a posture maintains that all convictions, even the most long-standing and dear, are subject to critical scrutiny and potentially to revision, reconstruction, or even rejection. It seeks to respond positively and appropriately to the situatedness of all human thought and therefore to embrace a principled hermeneutical pluralism. It also attempts to affirm that the ultimate authority in the church is not a particular source, whether Scripture, tradition, culture, or a particular doctrine or confession, but only the living God revealed in Jesus Christ. This means that human beings are always in a position of dependence and in need of grace with respect to epistemic relations with God. Attempts on the part of humans to seize control of these relations are all too common throughout the history of the church and, no matter how well intentioned, inevitably lead to forms of conceptual idolatry and oppression. We believe that missional hermeneutics can nurture an open and flexible approach that is in keeping with the local and contextual character of human knowledge.

A third posture of the missional hermeneutics we are proposing is closely related to the second. The commitment to resist foundationalism leads to a posture that is against totality. If missional hermeneutics is positively committed to the radical contextuality of intercultural hermeneutics, it stands in opposition to claims that any particular interpretive conclusions are universal for all times and places. This commitment arises from both cultural-anthropological and missiological considerations. From the perspective of cultural anthropology, this stance against totality is connected to the sociology of knowledge and the linguistic turn. Anthropologists maintain that humans do not view the world from an objective vantage point, but structure their world through the concepts they bring to it, particularly language. Human languages function as social conventions that describe the world in a variety of ways depending on the context of the speaker. No simple, one-to-one relationship exists between language and the world and thus no single linguistic description can serve to provide an objective conception of the so-called "real" world. Language structures our perceptions of reality and constitutes the world in which we live.

Anthropologists have discarded the older assumption that culture is a preexisting social-ordering force that is transmitted externally to members of a cultural group who in turn passively internalize it. They maintain that this view is mistaken in that it isolates culture from the ongoing social processes that produce and continually alter it. Culture is not an entity standing above or beyond human products and learned mental structures. In short, culture is not a thing. The modern understanding tended to focus on the idea of culture as that which integrates the various institutional expressions of social life and binds the individual to society. This focus on the integrative role of culture faces serious challenges.

Rather than exercising determinative power over people, culture is now conceived as the outcome and product of social interaction. Consequently, rather than being viewed as passive receivers, human beings are seen as the active creators of culture. Culture resides in a set of meaningful forms and symbols that, from the point of view of any particular individual, appear as largely given. Yet these forms are only meaningful because human minds have the ability to interpret them. This has led anthropologists to look at the interplay of cultural artifacts and human interpretation in the formation of meaning. They suggest that, contrary to the belief that meaning lies in signs or in the relations between them, meanings are bestowed by the users of signs. This does not mean, however, that individuals simply discover or make up cultural meanings on their own. Even the mental structures by which they interpret the world are developed through explicit teaching and implicit observation of others. The thrust of contemporary cultural anthropology leads to the conclusion that its primary concern lies in understanding the creation of cultural meaning as connected to world construction and identity formation.

This approach leads to an understanding of culture as socially constructed. The thesis of social constructionists is that, rather than inhabiting a prefabricated, given world, we live in a linguistically construed social-cultural world of our own creation. At the heart of the process whereby we construct our world is the imposition of some semblance of a meaningful order upon our variegated experiences. For the interpretive framework we employ in this task, we are dependent on the society in which we participate. In this manner, society mediates to us the cultural tools necessary for constructing our world. Although this constructed world gives the semblance of being a given, universal, and objective reality, it is actually an unstable structure that is constantly being challenged, deconstructed, reinterpreted, and reimagined.

We inhabit linguistically and socially constructed worlds to which our personal identities are intricately bound. The construction of these worlds, as well as the formation of personal identity, is an ongoing, dynamic, and fluid process, in which the forming and reforming of shared cultural meanings play a crucial role. To be human is to be embedded in culture and to participate in the process of interpretation and the creation of meaning as we reflect on and internalize the cultural symbols that we share with others in numerous conversations that shape our ever-shifting contexts.

In the face of these constantly shifting circumstances, we suggest that missional hermeneutics involves the ongoing interactions between the texts, cultures, social circumstances, and the experiences of different readers. These interactions call forth fresh efforts in listening to the voice of the Spirit speaking in and through the texts of Scripture, often with challenging results, especially for long entrenched positions that have the appearance of established orthodoxy. For instance, the current racial inequities in North America call forth fresh readings of the biblical texts. This inequity, along with the fear, poverty, and injustice it both reflects and produces, is contrary to the reign of God proclaimed by Jesus in the Gospels. He announced the coming of a world where everyone would have enough and no one would need to be afraid. He sent the church into the world as a sign, instrument, and foretaste of that intended reality. The implication of this calling requires the church to be intentionally antiracist in its witness to the gospel.

Tragically, the church has failed in its calling to bear such witness. In fact, the expansion of the church in history has often been an exercise in the extension of empire and its will to dominate. For example, Rome did not make Christianity its official religion in the fourth century in order to enable the church to critique and challenge its practices concerning the use and manifestation of power and privilege. Rather, the empire shaped the church to underwrite its own ends and give them divine sanction. This arrangement is known as Christendom, and its institutions remain with us in the present time. It has become increasingly clear that Western mission has traditionally been an Anglo-European church-centered enterprise and that the gospel has been passed on in the cultural shape of the Western church. One of the continuing manifestations of this tradition is the common assumption of a universal approach to theology—one right set of sources, one right method, and one right system of thought or doctrine.

Theology, however, does not function as a universal language. As we have noted, it is always a particular interpretation of revelation, Scripture, and tradition that reflects the goals, aspirations, and beliefs of a particular people, a particular community. As such, theology cannot speak for all. When it insists on doing so, and when this insistence is coupled with cultural and societal power, it becomes oppressive to those who do not share its values and outlooks, leaving them painfully disenfranchised.

In this way, the dominant theologies of North American history have contributed to the racism that permeates society. As many scholars have pointed out, theological reflection in the United States did not arise from the experiences and social realities of people of color. Rather, its character was determined by those who were so committed to its European and Enlightenment presumptions that they failed to question its conclusions of cultural supremacy that led to colonization, exploitation, extermination, and slavery for non-white people.

White American theologians across the ideological spectrum interpreted the gospel and the Christian faith from the perspective of the dominant cultural group. We interpreted the Bible and constructed theology in support of the political and social status quo, in spite of the voices crying out for more just and equitable treatment. We neglected these voices because of our deeply held beliefs and convictions, which took for granted the normativity of the white experience. We failed to recognize that other people, specifically non-white people, also had thoughts about God, Jesus, and the Bible—*thoughts that mattered.* If the church is to fulfill its obligation to bear an antiracist witness in the world, we must begin by surrendering the pretensions of a universally normative theology. Where we are unwilling to do this, we propagate forms of cultural, ethnic, and racial imperialism under the guise of Christian faith.

The failure to surrender these pretensions will continually undermine attempts at a truly antiracist witness in the church. This is because Christian faith will continue to be defined in ways that are governed by the outlooks characteristic of white experience and its cultural dominance. Antiracist witness cannot be achieved on these terms.

If a faithfully antiracist witness is to take hold and flourish in the church, we must be willing to subject the theological traditions of the white church to greater critical scrutiny and intentionally decenter them. Only in this way will we be in a position to take seriously the voices and experiences of others who have been marginalized for far too long. While this task of decentering the white theological tradition will be difficult and often painful to those of us who have been formed and privileged by it, such a process is necessary for the antiracist witness of the church.

For the sake of the gospel and the community that is called to bear living witness to it, we must in humility consider the interests and concerns of others before our own in keeping with the example of the Lord of the church, who "emptied himself" for us (see Phil 2:6–8). This kenotic example is always relevant as we seek to become more faithful participants in God's liberating, missional purposes.

Conclusion

The vision for missional hermeneutics that we have proposed in the last three chapters reflects our attempt to make explicit what we suggest has remained largely implicit in much of the conversation about missional interpretation to this point. Specifically, we hope to see missional hermeneutics become an explicitly and holistically liberative approach to biblical interpretation, consonant in fact with the purposes of God. In part, this is because we believe that this emerging subfield of interpretation would do well consistently to adopt and reflect a range of contemporary postmodern philosophical and interdisciplinary insights that have profoundly liberative implications not only for biblical interpretation but also Christian life and witness more broadly. While no philosophical paradigm can characterize and capture all of reality accurately and completely, we are convinced that Enlightenment modernity's tendencies toward reductionism, reification, and control obligate us to engage with the realities of divine mystery and biblical ambiguity in new ways, even when our modernist tendencies lead us to experience mystery and ambiguity as unsettling. Ultimately, although cultivating openness to difference and humility about what we can truly know may be unnerving and challenging, we find the process and its results to be liberating—and, as our proposal seeks to suggest, faithful to the nature and testimony of Scripture itself.

In any event, our particular proposal depends upon and develops various threads within the missional hermeneutics conversation that we have to be found especially sensitive to and reflective of both the dynamic and untamable nature of the triune God and the character of Scripture itself—threads that strike us as especially hopeful, energizing, and, ultimately, liberating.

As we propose and advocate for an explicitly liberative approach to missional hermeneutics, we humbly want to acknowledge and give credit to the many voices within a variety of liberationist theological traditions who have influenced and deepened our understanding of the gospel—and thus of the *missio Dei*.[6] Gustavo Gutiérrez, for example, whose ground-breaking *A Theology of Liberation* heralded and inaugurated an outpouring of powerful and sustained theological reflection throughout Latin America (and would be joined by similarly liberative Asian and African theologies), called readers across the globe to read and interpret the Bible with and from the perspective of the poor and oppressed.[7] Gutiérrez and many others have exhorted readers to see that the God of the Bible does not separate matters of contemporary economic and societal justice from the "spiritual" dynamics of the gospel, recognizing, for example, that God steadfastly opposes the exploitation and dehumanization of the vulnerable and marginalized by powerful elites that the poor in Latin America continue to experience in our own day. Latin American liberation theologians remind us that the salvation offered and effected by the biblical God is comprehensive—unmasking, engaging, and defeating every force and structure that shackles and dehumanizes.

Relatedly, and, for North Americans, in even more culturally and historically direct ways, feminist, black, and womanist theologians—among others—have explored not only the liberative dynamics operative in biblical texts themselves, but also many fresh and liberative insights that can be gleaned by reading texts through contextually located lenses. By interpretively centering the experiences of oppressed and marginalized peoples, these readers have demonstrated again and again that divine liberation always reaches further and more fully than traditional theological reflection (characteristic of privileged white, Western male interpreters) has tended to imagine. In short, liberationist theologies challenge and encourage us to see more clearly the holistic purposiveness of the God of all liberation, which, as Gutiérrez reminds us, takes us to the very heart of the divine mission and, derivatively, to the mission of God's people: "the scope and gravity of the process of liberation is such that to ponder

---

6. Among those whose thought has deeply influenced and broadened our understanding of liberation is famed Brazilian educator Paulo Freire. His classic work, *Pedagogy of the Oppressed* (originally published in 1970; more recently, see *Pedagogy of the Oppressed*, 50th anniversary ed.) while not a work of Christian theology—and written from a socioeconomic and political context quite different from our own—is a tremendously important analysis of power dynamics and the quest for liberative social change through conscientization and engaged praxis. Freire's guidance is deeply helpful for engaging with biblical texts in terms of the liberative missional hermeneutics we are proposing.

7. Gutiérrez, *Theology of Liberation*.

its significance is really to examine the meaning of Christianity itself and the mission of the Church in the world."[8]

The kind of liberative missional hermeneutics that we envision has learned from and drawn on important insights and themes from a variety of liberationist theological interpreters and traditions to which we are indebted. What follows is especially, though by no means exclusively, characteristic of Latin American liberation theology.[9] Other liberative traditions (e.g., black, feminist, womanist) have drawn on, modified, and supplemented some of these basic insights.

As a God of love, justice, and liberation, the God of the Bible does not remain neutral in the face of poverty, oppression, and marginalization; doing so would serve to support the powers that enact such injustice. Rather, God engages the struggle, taking up the cause of the poor and marginalized. If this is how God operates, the same should obviously be true of the church. Within the Catholic theological tradition, this theological prioritization of the economically vulnerable and marginalized has become known as the "preferential option for the poor." While the insight that God takes sides in situations of injustice is a crucial contribution of Latin American liberation theology, we note that it is already a widespread biblical theme.

Liberationist theologies of all kinds challenge us to remember that power and privilege function as blinders that keep us from seeing, acknowledging, and responding to much of what is actually happening—in our lives and communities as well as in the texts we read. Consequently, if those of us who read from positions of power and privilege hope to experience more of the liberative good news that has been offered and is available to all of us, we must read with and learn from those who see and experience what we do not. Given the biblical God's presence with the poor, marginalized, and vulnerable, liberation theologies suggest that those communities actually begin from privileged a location as they seek to experience and understand God. Liberationist theological traditions do not "invent" a God who attends to the vulnerable and exploited; rather, these traditions recognize that those who read from such locations tend to see in biblical texts what escapes notice from those who are aligned with power and privilege.

8. Gutiérrez, *Theology of Liberation*, 143.

9. For a helpful summary of Latin American liberation theology, in particular—which helps inform the paragraphs that follow—see Smith, *Emergence of Liberation Theology*, 27–50.

A central feature of liberative theologies, therefore, is their praxis orientation. Liberationist approaches refuse to separate theology as intellectual theory from its concrete, practical application in daily life—as if biblical interpretation and theological reflection could (and should) be developed in abstraction before being put tangibly into operation in specific contexts. Such a theory-to-application model has often been characteristic of traditional white, Euro-American, male theologizing. For liberationist theologies, however, such bifurcation between theory and practice regularly serves to reinforce existing power relationships and thus maintain the social and intellectual status quo. Liberative traditions thus advocate a praxis model of theologizing, in which concrete action in the world and theological reflection about that activity take place in a cyclical and mutually informing fashion. Abstract theory does not simply get "applied," as it were, but concrete experience on the ground informs theological reflection, which continues to inform future action, and so forth. A praxis orientation democratizes power relationships, serving to liberate those whose experiences and struggles, voices and wisdom are often overlooked. It requires that theological reflection take place within and informed by contemporary social experience and realities on the ground. This is precisely what we are advocating when we speak of missional hermeneutics as a form of embedded, located interpretation.

In various ways, liberationist traditions shine a light on the reality that injustices so often associated with power and privilege are not societal givens ordained by God, but are reflections of human frailty and sinfulness. Latin American liberation theology, for example, has long emphasized the necessity of addressing disparities of economic and social power to reveal more fully the liberative character of the gospel and the full flourishing of God's creation. While many North Americans tend reflexively to resist the notion of inescapable opposition between groups (e.g., along class lines in Latin American liberation theology), such resistance does not negate reality.

Liberation theologies remind us that sin and its effects are never merely personal and interpersonal, but rather thoroughly embedded and manifested in our social and societal structures. As a consequence, to address human sinfulness requires thoroughgoing repair in all dimensions of life and society, and not simply the reception of individualized "spiritual" absolution from God. To reckon with and make reparation for the dehumanizing effects of sin—such as poverty, exploitation, marginalization, sexism, patriarchy, and racism (in all of their interpersonal and structural forms)—will always require more than mere tinkering around the edges of our problems and injustices. For too long, those of us with power and privilege have been complicit in sinful structures, failing to recognize the extent to which we dehumanize others (and, in the process, of ourselves) while benefiting, directly and indirectly, from the status quo. Black liberationist and womanist theological traditions call North American Christians out for our unwillingness to explore and acknowledge the extent to which American culture and American Christianity are steeped in the assumptions, norms, and practices of white supremacy. Many of us in the white community bristle at the notion that "racism" is something deeper and more insidious than a personal character flaw. The problem is that sin—in its myriad forms—is much more of a problem than the powerful and privileged have often recognized, and rooting it out necessitates struggle and enduring change that are revolutionary in character. Liberationist traditions thus stress the critically significant role and function of all forms of power, and the importance of recognizing, acknowledging, and sharing it such that all humans experience liberative opportunities to thrive and flourish.

Liberationist theological traditions also point to the liberative example and function of Jesus, who taught and exemplified embodied, self-giving love and mercy. However we understand the incarnation, there can be no doubt that in affirming divine engagement with humanity in Jesus of Nazareth, we are claiming that God is deeply familiar with human realities, including oppression and marginalization. His life clarifies and dignifies our own embodied experiences, and his death and resurrection herald an ultimate liberation from sin and death. Liberationist theologies also remind us that the experience of salvation is never *merely* a spiritual, individualized, or future matter, but rather is always something that engages the entirety of our embodied and material, relational and communal, and present needs and realities. Everything that is happening in our lives and in our world matters to God, and thus it should matter to God's people: again, the purposes of God—the divine mission—must inform the missional identity and activity of the church.

Many other themes from liberationist theological traditions could be identified. We hope that those we have mentioned briefly will be sufficient to illustrate and emphasize that a liberative missional hermeneutics as we envision it is informed and shaped by several influential and often deeply salutary trajectories of liberative theological praxis. While missional hermeneutics need not adopt in an uncritical fashion everything that liberationist traditions pass on, it is important that we acknowledge how much these theological approaches are helping to foster the liberation of dehumanized and suffering peoples and, in many cases, of Scripture itself.

Whether or not readers share our hopes for the kind of postmodern, liberative missional hermeneutics that we have proposed, we believe that missional hermeneutics, generally speaking, undoubtedly offers a helpful approach for biblical interpretation. Characterized by an intentional focus upon who God is, what God cares about, and what God is doing—and how God's people are called to participate in those divine purposes—missional hermeneutics as it has been theorized, practiced, and debated provides a reading posture that consciously attends to the biblical formation of contemporary readers while never losing sight of the fact that, from a biblical perspective, the church's mission, properly speaking, is always derivative of God's nature and activity. Reading Scripture so as to discern divine purposes and how reading communities may participate faithfully within them remains a noteworthy interpretive contribution of missional hermeneutics, whether readers adopt every facet of our vision for the movement going forward, or not.

While we are not claiming that missional hermeneutics is solely or uniquely able to liberate Scripture, we do find that its focus on the interpretive import of divine purposes—and human participation within them—fosters a hermeneutical posture especially attentive to the wide and holistic scope of God's salvific intentionality and activity. Missional hermeneutics assumes that there is always *more* to what God is up to, always *more* to the good news than we have grasped, always *more* to the ways in which we are being liberated from everything that keeps us and the rest of creation in bondage. May the God of all liberation, who chooses to invite us to participate in those divine purposes, find us faithful in our derivative mission.

CHAPTER 7

The Practice of Missional Hermeneutics

IN THIS FINAL CHAPTER, we seek to get a bit more concrete, as we now consider what missional interpretation looks like, practically speaking. Once we move beyond broad generalities and affirmations about the mission of God—and derivatively, the participation of God's people within those divine purposes—how, specifically, does missional interpretation relate to the exegetical and hermeneutical processes involved in engaging with individual portions of Scripture, such as a short pericope that might serve as the focus of a particular Bible study or sermon?

What follows, of course, will be brief—more suggestive and illustrative than prescriptive. As we begin, it bears repeating once again that what missional hermeneutics provides is a framework or posture for interpretation, not an especially unique or precise methodology. Above all, missional hermeneutics involves approaching Scripture with curiosity and openness, seeking to explore how it illuminates and furthers the *missio Dei*. Such an interpretive posture quite naturally engenders particular kinds of questions—missionally located questions that seek to elicit iterative reflection and increasing clarity about both God's mission and the interpretive community's participatory vocation within those divine purposes. Remember that missional interpretation readily embraces whatever discrete interpretive methodologies that may help to highlight and illuminate those two concerns. Interpreters interested in engaging in missional interpretation can and should continue to engage in the wide and expanding range of historical-critical exploration, literary analysis, and perspectival approaches rooted in interpreters' identities and experiences. Missional interpretation does not override or compete with those approaches so much as it offers a vantage point within which those interpretive issues may be explored in fresh and exciting ways, such that the intrinsic, formative, purposive concerns of biblical texts naturally come to fore.

It is crucial to recognize that while evangelism (in its myriad forms) is an important and integral part of the church's mission, that mission cannot be reduced to or narrowly equated with evangelism. Therefore, missional interpretation is *not* primarily about finding texts in the Bible that seem to relate to things like "evangelism" or "outreach" or the geographical expansion of Christianity around the world (i.e., things related to "mission," *traditionally understood*). That traditional approach essentially assumes that we already know what mission is (often understood in terms that are nearly synonymous with evangelistic outreach and expansion), and that we open the Bible to find things in it that are consistent with those traditional assumptions and definitions of mission. Again, by contrast, missional interpretation avoids such traditional and ultimately reductionistic notions of mission, focusing more generally upon divine purposiveness—and human participation within those purposes—so as to derive an understanding of mission from the Bible itself rather than by importing our own definitions into Scripture.

There are, of course, a variety of ways to "get into" a text missionally. The three lenses of interpretation (and the various "streams" within missional hermeneutics) that we highlighted in the second chapter serve as broad frameworks within which to begin to explore a given passage. While there are certainly valid reasons for beginning to engage a passage from each of these vantage points, we especially advocate starting with the located context within which interpretation is currently taking place. That is because the contemporary missional *location* of readers and reading communities is crucial for liberative interpretation.

In other words, we must pay attention to what have been called "the signs of the times"—to what's happening "on the ground," as it were, in our contemporary moment. In order to avoid shackling Scripture, we must be honest, humble, and courageous enough to come to the text open to seeing and hearing new things, in part by approaching Scripture with conscious awareness of our socially located perspectives, especially as communities of faith embedded in concrete temporal and social contexts. Those contexts matter. We must be deeply wary of interpreting the Bible in supposedly generic, "a-contextual," universalizing ways—in ways that imply that our contextualized interpretations are fully and equally applicable "for all times and places," as it were. When we interpret the Bible "generally," without adequate attention to the context within which interpretation is taking place, we tend to shackle Scripture's ability to speak in new and fresh ways. We can end up focusing on timeless affirmations and principles that may reflect the concerns of a particular interpretive moment but that may leave us without eyes to see and ears to hear what the Spirit may be seeking to communicate through Scripture in different contexts.

There is a strong presumption in missional hermeneutics that the biblical text—however it may be investigated and engaged exegetically—has tremendous contemporary relevance and merits serious and sustained reflection within contextually located reading communities today. This is not to suggest that every biblical passage is fully and directly relevant for contemporary readers—or that all biblical texts are equally authoritative. To say those things would, once again, amount to shackling Scripture by viewing and evaluating it from within a reductively rigid, rational, and narrow perspective. Still, the Bible undoubtedly has critically important things to say—and questions to ask—about what is going on in the world and in our lives, individually and collectively, right now—and in *every* now. Considering such located concerns is, for us, at the heart of missional interpretation of Scripture. Again, missional hermeneutics is fundamentally about reflecting on the Bible so as to discern, through the guidance and inspiration of the Spirit of God, what God is up to and how we as the people of God are being called and invited into participation within those divine purposes in our concrete contexts and circumstances. Such concerns are always matters of deep, interpretive relevance.

In order to exemplify how missional hermeneutics functions, we will consider three texts—Matthew 18:21–35; and, more briefly, Genesis 38 and Leviticus 25—that have economic dimensions and implications. We turn to these passages not because economic dynamics are the only considerations that matter for a missional hermeneutic, but rather because many Christians today see such issues as largely extrinsic to divine purposes (and thus extrinsic to the church's participation in God's mission)—despite the fact that the Bible itself repeatedly undermines such assumptions.

It is important to note that Scripture does not often distinguish between spiritual and material concerns—or sharply prioritize the former over the latter—as is common in much of North American Christianity. Many understand the gospel to be so fundamentally about what are deemed to be "spiritual" matters (e.g., personal salvation; individual holiness) that other forms of liberation (such as economic and other forms of societal justice) are considered secondary and incidental, if not altogether irrelevant. We submit, however, that any notion of a gospel focused narrowly on the salvation of individual souls in preparation for a heavenly afterlife represents a decidedly incomplete picture of biblical testimony. In Scripture, God's liberative purposes—and thus the good news concerning what God is up to, especially in and through Jesus the Christ—is all-encompassing in its liberative power: material and physical no less than spiritual, social and communal no less than personal. There are no bounds to God's liberation. As followers of Jesus, we are called to participate within larger divine purposes—and thus in *all* of the ways in which God's liberative good news can free us and the whole of creation from myriad forms of bondage—material, physical, social, and spiritual. That is why we are advocating an explicitly liberative missional hermeneutics. As we read Scripture from a missional posture, aspects of the biblical text that our social locations lead us to overlook or ignore are in fact those that we must revisit again and again.

Moving Beyond Calculation:
A Missional Reading of Matt 18:21–35

Matthew 18:21–35 is a fascinating passage for thinking about human participation in divine purposes, and it provides a good example of how traditional attempts to locate "mission"—in terms of evangelistic outreach—in the Bible differ from what we mean by missional hermeneutics. There is little or nothing in Matt 18:21–35 that has anything to do with evangelism (or other "mission-oriented" things, traditionally understood) beyond the faith community. Indeed, this passage is entirely oriented to what happens *within* the church itself.[1] The text begins in v. 21 with a query from Peter: "Lord, if another member of the church [Greek: 'my brother'] sins against me, how often should I forgive?" Again, from a traditional perspective, this

---

1. Matthew is the only one of the four Gospels in which Jesus is described as twice referring specifically to "the church" (Gk: *ekklesia*) in 18:17, in the passage (vv. 15–20) that immediately precedes 18:21–35 (the text under consideration here).

text seemingly has nothing to do with "mission." Viewed from the perspective of the *missio Dei*, however, this passage reveals much about divine purposiveness and, by extension, the mission of the church.

We all come to this text as located readers. Let us begin by acknowledging some of the contextually located dynamics that characterize us, no less than Peter. Each of us knows that offering forgiveness can be challenging. And, culturally speaking, it is not always clear what authentic forgiveness involves. Many of us have been taught that forgiveness amounts to forgetting—simplistically "moving on from"—what has been hurtful, even if we have not adequately come to terms with the pain and grief unleashed by the original offense.

Those of us who claim the mantle of "Christian" believe that we have been forgiven by a God who does not hold us to account in a manner commensurate with our conduct. But we also live in a world characterized by transactional and meritocratic moral economies, leading us to believe that treating wrongdoing with mercy may be naïve, foolish, and ineffectual. Indeed, most of us have been socioculturally formed to operate by moral calculation, and in ways that suggest that we doubt the possibility—not to mention the reality—of complete forgiveness.

As human beings, we are born calculators. As we interpret the world around us, we analyze and evaluate, taking note of and acting in response to data that we gather and process. Our moral discernments are regularly rooted in, related to, and reflective of the calculations we make. Indeed, most of us simply presuppose the necessity of calculation in moral decision-making. But is it possible that some of our calculating tendencies can actually *hinder* our ability to understand—and participate in—what Jesus was trying to communicate about the reign of God? Matthew 18:21–35 illustratively suggests the importance of moving *beyond calculation*, particularly with regard to forgiveness within the community of faith (and, presumably, in contexts beyond that community as well).

As human beings, we hurt and are hurt by others. We engage in moral comparison, judging and holding grudges. True forgiveness is always challenging—both to give and to receive. To interpret Matt 18:21–35 *missionally* necessitates that we reckon with the ways in which it cuts against the grain of our culturally sanctioned assumptions and behaviors. We must acknowledge that we are embedded—*missionally located*—in contexts that understand radical mercy and forgiveness to be challenging, counterintuitive, and countercultural. Missionally, then, we must come to this text as located readers and communities who are engaged in the world (in one way or another, and to one degree or another), seeking to discern more fully and faithfully what God is up to—and how God is inviting us to participate more fully and faithfully in those divine purposes.

A significant first step in missional interpretation relative to this passage might involve reflecting thoughtfully and carefully on the painful, concrete challenges that conflict and forgiveness represent in our located contexts—and how these tangible, real phenomena affect our daily, ongoing participation within the larger purposes of God. Again, we are talking primarily about a posture that we take as interpreters in relation to the biblical text. Asking serious and thoughtful, missionally located questions—questions open-ended enough to allow for responses and conclusions deeper than and beyond those we may initially anticipate—will be crucial in this regard. A nearly endless variety of such questions could be posed. Coming to the biblical text with a missional posture does not mean that there is a specific list of questions that must be asked of every passage. Rather, it means that we come to Scripture asking any and all questions that may illuminate God's purposes and our calling to participate within them. Perhaps we might imagine that one of the roles of God's Spirit in our midst is to shape, form, and inspire us to ask questions of the text and of ourselves—and to attend more fully to the questions, explicit and implicit alike, that the text is posing for us—such that our faithful participation in the missio Dei will be furthered and deepened.

With regard to Matt 18:21–35, we might begin by asking the following kinds of located, missional questions that are engendered by our own contextual realities: What kinds of conflicts take place within, among, and beyond our communities, and what difficulties do those conflicts pose for our authentic and faithful participation within the purposes of God? How do we currently think about and experience divine forgiveness, and how can we more fully understand the role of such forgiveness within the missio Dei? In what ways do we find forgiveness challenging—especially given our contextual-cultural formation, and how do we manifest those challenges in the ways that we participate—both faithfully and unfaithfully—within God's larger mission? Do we understand the specific opportunities we have to offer or receive forgiveness in terms of larger divine purposes—God's mission—and, if so, how? If not, why not? In what ways do we currently practice forgiveness—or fail to do so—in concert with what God is doing in the world? In light of Matt 18:21–35, how do we currently participate in unhelpful and unhealthy calculation relative to forgiveness, and what would it look like to move beyond such moral calculation toward more faithful participation in divine purposes? Many other missionally located questions will likely occur to us as we start to ask them, especially as we do so with others in and beyond our communities of faith.

As we begin to reflect thoughtfully on forgiveness in Matt 18:21–35 relative to our contemporary missional locatedness, we can also explore a wide range of missional questions about what we find *in the text itself* and about what may contextually lay *behind it*. Again, what makes such questions "missional" is not so much that they manifest a particular format or content as that they are inspired by and seek to foster an interpretive posture oriented toward the divine mission and faithful participation within it. Missionally, we will certainly want to explore how Peter's questions (Matt 18:21) and Jesus's parabolic response (vv. 22–35) reorient our tendencies toward moral calculation as those who are invited and called into participation in the reign of heaven.

In Matt 18:21, in the wider context of Jesus's teaching on wrongdoing, repentance, and forgiveness within the kingdom community (note Jesus's dual references to "the church" in v. 17), Peter approaches Jesus with a question, followed by a suggested answer in the form of a second query: "Lord, how often should I forgive if my brother sins against me? As many as seven times?" Notice that Peter presupposes the necessity of forgiveness, agreeing with Jesus that it is an imperative for a healthy community. His initial question is not about *whether* one should forgive, but rather *how many times.*

It is unlikely that Peter is proposing a merely theoretical, theological conundrum to see what Jesus will do with it, as Jesus's opponents in the Gospel narratives are often wont to do. Rather, we may imagine that Peter has a specific disciple in mind with whom he has experienced conflict: "Jesus, how many times (or, perhaps, 'how often') do I have to forgive *that guy?*" Again, Peter's initial question is not about whether or not to forgive, but rather how many times it should happen. At the heart of Peter's questions is a significant moral calculation.

If the basic concern about the need for forgiveness within a community is not theoretical, neither is Peter's specific suggestion regarding its frequency. It is unlikely that we are to understand his second question—"As many as seven times?" (v. 21)—as reflecting a stingy reluctance to offer much forgiveness. Given the frustration and pain that ongoing mistreatment by a "brother" [or sister] in the community would undoubtedly entail, Matthew probably intends that we read Peter's question as coming from a place of relative generosity. Offering direct, individualized, and iterative forgiveness in a small community would certainly become challenging for a repeatedly aggrieved member. Peter is proposing a fairly magnanimous level of forgiveness. Seven times would require a lot of the person offering forgiveness and would demonstrate a sincere willingness to establish and maintain a healthy community. Indeed, the biblically symbolic nature of the number seven, emphasizing, for example, completion and perfection, lends support to the idea that Peter's concern is probably coming from a "good place," as it were.

Jesus's initial response to Peter—"Not seven times, but, I tell you, seventy-seven times" (v. 22)[2]—suggests, however, that the disciple has not even begun to understand and enact the nature and scope of forgiveness that communal participation in "the reign of heaven" would actually entail. Despite his apparently generous spirit, Peter seems to have engaged in a form of moral and relational calculation that Jesus ultimately intends to root out among his followers.

Lest we suppose that Jesus simply replaces a smaller number with a much larger, but equally specific one, we must think carefully about what his response implies. Imagine if Peter were to take Jesus's instructions literally, beginning to count every one of the times he needed to forgive each of his brothers and sisters in the budding community gathered around the messiah. It would be easy enough for Peter to enumerate (and to remember where he was in the count toward) seven offers of forgiveness, but it would be far more challenging to do so for as many as seventy-seven pardons. What kind of forgiveness would Peter be offering if he were trying to keep an accurate count all the way to seventy-seven ("1, 2, 3 . . . 23, 24, 25 . . . 38, 39, 40 . . .")? Cataloging every instance in which a brother or sister had wronged him, thereby keeping an accurate count of each time a pardon was necessary—whether up to seven or even seventy-seven—would not reflect much forgiveness at all. Indeed, it would essentially amount to an intentional attempt on Peter's part *not* to release the brother or sister needing forgiveness from the debt (by literally continuing to count it against him or her), even as he effectively applauded himself for demonstrating such over-the-top generosity in offering such iterative "forgiveness."

Jesus's response to Peter—"Not seven times, but, I tell you, seventy-seven times"—is best understood not simply as a command that Peter forgive

---

2. The best reading of this text is "seventy-seven" rather "seventy times seven."

others far more than seven times, but even more as a thoroughgoing deconstruction of the human tendency to fixate on others' indebtedness (while at the same time valorizing one's supposed willingness to forgive). Jesus does not literally want Peter to count to seventy-seven (though that number would presumably symbolize even greater "perfection" than seven). Rather, Jesus wants Peter to stop counting at all, to refrain from ever calculating how much forgiveness (i.e., "how many times," or, perhaps "how often") he would be willing to offer in the first place.

This point is dramatically underscored through the parable that Jesus narrates in vv. 23–35. Immediately after telling Peter to forgive, in effect, without limit ("seventy-seven times"), Jesus launches into an illustrative story that highlights the illogical foolishness of mental calculation regarding repetitive offers of forgiveness. Interestingly, Matthew frames Peter's question in v. 21 as involving interpersonal forgiveness; there is no suggestion that the disciple's question has anything to do with financial or economic matters. And yet Matthew describes Jesus as linking the parable in vv. 23–35 (see v. 22: "For this reason . . .")—with its explicitly economic considerations—to the issue of forgiveness. While forgiveness is obviously relevant in many situations that have nothing to do with economics, the economic character of Jesus's response to Peter here is noteworthy. The parable is more than a simple illustration of what happens in the absence of forgiveness; indeed, the economic dynamics in the parable seem to underscore that the human tendency toward moral calculation is itself problematic.

Jesus tells Peter that "the reign of heaven" is comparable to a scenario involving stock first-century characters (e.g., kings, slaves) and relatively familiar situations (e.g., indebtedness and the inability to escape it). Although some of the details of the story are comically improbable, this story is nevertheless relatable and relevant for those familiar with the economic context of the larger Roman Empire, in which debilitating indebtedness and the varied forms in which freedom could be lost as a result of it were *not* merely theoretical possibilities. Jesus uses an extreme, albeit ostensibly this-worldly situation in order to illustrate that forgiveness beyond calculation is not only entirely possible, but precisely the kind of reasoning and conduct that characterizes life in "the reign of heaven." Indeed, such forgiveness would amount to an example of living already—right now—within the framework of a revolutionary economy characteristic of a divine (rather than human) empire.

The astronomical amount of the first slave's debt (more than 150,000 *years* of wages) is beyond repayable, even over many lifetimes. He could not possibly have ever *needed* an original loan of such overflowing abundance, nor could he have possibly used more than a tiny portion of the overwhelmingly large amount loaned to him. If the king is to be understood in any sense as representing God (see, e.g., v. 35), the outrageously lavish credit afforded the first slave takes on rich theological symbolism. The fact that he has already squandered more than someone could possibly have spent across multiple lifetimes drips with suggestive and unsettling theological irony. We must not miss the fact that the parable not only highlights the man's inability to repay the debt he owes; the story also suggests that he has entirely squandered a gigantic loan that should have enabled him to live large for many lifetimes.

The king cancels the first slave's debt—for us, an unimaginably foolish and counterintuitive decision, but one that is meant to illustrate reality itself, understood from the vantage point of a divine economy characterized by uncalculating abundance and mercy. In effect, the king forgives the slave more than seventy-seven times all at once. Seemingly oblivious to the shocking enormity of what has just happened, the slave then shamelessly proceeds to calculate how much he has to gain by demanding repayment on a far more quotidian loan owed to him by a fellow slave. His shameful behavior ends up getting him thrown into prison after all.

In the context of the Gospel narrative, Jesus tells this parable in order to highlight the extreme foolishness of calculating how much forgiveness one should be willing and prepared to provide. Jesus seems to be suggesting that offering forgiveness liberally and without calculation can open his followers up, in the here and now, to a kind of abundant and overflowing communal life together that actually reflects and embodies the reign of heaven within which the king's strange and unconventional economic reasoning begins to make sense. As readers, we are invited to recognize that calculating how often to forgive fails to bring such a flourishing life; rather, doing so reinforces in us a scarcity mindset, in which we imagine that the unfathomable abundance that has been provided for us amounts to little more than an enormous, unpayable debt. When we live primarily by moral calculation, it is entirely possible—indeed, it is essentially inevitable—that we will miss out on the incalculable abundance that has been provided for us.

The parable ends with what appears, at first glance, to be a shocking reversal from the king. The recklessly merciful monarch now sentences the "wicked slave" (v. 32) to be tortured "until he would repay his entire debt" (v. 34). As we get to the end of the parable, we might feel compelled to exclaim, *Wait a minute!* Was not the king initially enacting and advocating uncalculated, iterative forgiveness? Why does he suddenly reverse course and refuse to forgive the slave again?

Perhaps the point is that what the king cannot countenance—what is unforgivably "wicked" in his eyes—is to fail to pass along to others the kinds of mercy that one has already received. Having been shown nearly unimaginable forgiveness, the first slave refused to treat a fellow debtor with similar compassion and mercy. Still, the harshness of the king's about-face is striking. Since the slave will never be able repay his enormous, original debt, he is effectively banished to everlasting torture. A cursory, traditionalist reading might, in allegorical fashion, connect this reference to punishment with eternal damnation. The narrative would thus theologically illustrate the horrible, enduring, spiritual price that human beings can expect to pay for failing to forgive others. Perhaps Matthew's inclusion of Jesus's concluding comment—"So my heavenly Father will also do to every one of you, if you do not forgive your brother or sister from your heart" (v. 35)—could be understood as support for that interpretation. While the eternal repercussions of unmerciful behavior *may* be something that Jesus is trying to get across, a quite different and deeply liberative reading might better connect the entirety of the passage together.

Again, Peter's initial questions presupposed the need to forgive repetitively. And in the context of Matthew's Gospel, his queries are contextually located within the ongoing life of an emergent community of faith. Perhaps we should be cautious about putting too much emphasis on eternal punishment in our reading of the parable. Something more immediate and quotidian may be at issue.

Notice that both of the enslaved debtors are forgiven by the king. Although each of them belongs to the king's community, the first slave treats the second in a way that is completely incommensurate with his own treatment by their merciful master. Perhaps the reference to torture at the end of the parable has less to do with eternal punishment than it does with the ongoing life of God's people, a community invited into—and called to bear contemporary witness to—the possibilities of living within a "reign" characterized by the values, priorities, and purposes of the king "of heaven."

A community characterized by hard-heartedness, judgmentalism, and retribution will struggle to experience, let alone to embody, an economy of incalculable mercy. Perhaps the king's rage—and the punishment he exacts—should be understood in terms of what in fact happens in our relationships, within the community of faith as well as beyond it. Consider: when we refuse to forgive someone else, who experiences the most "torture"? When we hold grudges, judging others for things that, to one degree or another, we are also guilty of—when we fail to forgive—who continues to suffer? Think of whose stomachs remain in knots and whose minds stay unsettled when we refuse to release others from their debts to us. Does not the failure to forgive often leave us feeling "tortured"?[3]

Jesus advocates mercy beyond calculation ("seventy-seven times") as a tangible (albeit endlessly challenging) facet of kingdom life together in community. Indeed, a commitment to iterative forgiveness is undoubtedly both a prerequisite and ongoing requirement for participation in the kind of "heavenly" community for which Jesus is forming his followers—including Peter and each of us. The parable suggests that the only way that each of Jesus's followers can "repay" their "entire debt" is to forgive others, truly and iteratively, without any forms of moral calculation that owe more to our human economic logics rooted in scarcity than to the abundantly merciful and gracious conduct of the king.[4]

So, again, what does it mean to read this parable missionally? As we have noted, it is clear that the parable is not concerned with the geographical or numerical expansion of the Christian community through evangelistic (e.g., "missionary") outreach beyond the bounds of the community. But it does point to the purposiveness of God, which we have described in terms of the *missio Dei*—and to the implications for the mission of the community of faith.

In Matt 18:21–35, Jesus is teaching his followers, through a conversation with Peter, about God's reign. It is clear that mercy and forgiveness are key to who God is, what God cares about, and what God and is doing in the world. God's "economy" operates quite differently from the moral and economic logics of human empires. In that sense, this parable takes

---

3. We are not suggesting here that forgiveness is limited to psychological dynamics, or that victims should ever be forced or "guilted" into forgiving their victimizers. See Maria Mayo's treatment of this passage in *Limits of Forgiveness*, 47–96.

4. This should not be understood as reflecting a form of "works righteousness." Unlike much of later Protestant theology, Matthew's Gospel is decidedly comfortable emphasizing the concrete, behavioral demands of gospel faith.

us toward the very heart of the gospel of a purposive God, a missional God. Missionally, we can seek to find ourselves in both Peter's questions and within the parable that Jesus tells. We must begin to reckon with the differences between God's uncalculating mercy, on the one hand, and our own, often quite calculated approaches to forgiveness, on the other. We are encouraged to reflect upon and actively explore what it would look like, in concert with God's enduring and purposeful mercy, to embody more faithfully a pattern of forgiveness consistent with the values and priorities of the reign of heaven.

Of course, a missional interpretive posture is not necessary for many of the exegetical observations we have made. Traditional methods can get us to most of them. But a missional posture *does* make a significant difference. To read this text missionally is to presuppose that, in one way or another, the text can be understood to communicate something about God and God's purposes—and, further, that it may provide at least some insight regarding human participation in that divine mission. While other approaches to the text may explore such things, missional hermeneutics is explicitly and intentionally oriented toward participatory engagement with and within God's missional purposes. Missional interpretation thus goes beyond traditional forms of hermeneutical inquiry, including some contemporary forms of scholarly theological interpretation.[5] It involves more than moral and theological reflection, moves beyond matters of denominational character and identity, and may both affirm and potentially reorient creedal affirmations.[6]

5. For an insightful consideration of the issues, see McKenzie, "Missional Hermeneutics as Theological Hermeneutic."

6. Elizabeth A. Johnson's observations are helpful here. She reminds us that all responsible and legitimate God-talk must acknowledge that "the reality of the living God is an ineffable mystery beyond all telling." Indeed, "like the sea which cannot be drunk dry, God surpasses whatever we can understand and account for in terms of our human categories" (*Quest for the Living God*, 17). A consequence of the reality that God is uncontainable and indescribable is that "no expression for God can be taken literally. None. Our language is like a finger pointing to the moon, not the moon itself. To equate the finger with the moon or to look at the finger and not perceive the moon is to fall into error. Never to be taken literally, human words about God proceed by way of indirection" (18). So, we can speak approximately of God by analogy, yes, but as Johnson points out, "analogy . . . affirms, negates, and then negates that affirmation itself." She illustrates, for example: "God is good; but God is not good the way creatures are good; but God is good in a supereminent way as Source of all that is good" (18). To refer to God as good by way of analogy can never be more than a weak approximation of divine reality. That is the best we can do as human beings.

Simply put, we can ask missional questions of this biblical text—and every other one—in order to explore the nature, shape, character, and implications of God's mission, including how those factors relate to the participation of God's people within divine purposes (both within the Bible and in subsequent generations). Obviously, such questions can go in various directions—for example, toward the biblical canon as a whole, toward specific biblical documents, and toward particular passages within those documents.

With regard to the entire biblical canon, we might ask whether and to what extent a robust notion of mission, particularly in terms of divine and ecclesial purposes, is discernible. Similarly, we can ask about how biblical documents and particular passages within them not only *reflect* wider biblical indications of the *missio Dei* but also *illuminate* aspects of those divine purposes. For example, we can and should ask how Matt 18:21–35 fits within the larger biblical *story* of God's purposiveness. How does it relate to wider canonical indications of God's mission? Does the passage reflect a consistent emphasis within Scripture, or does it have a unique or otherwise rare character that should be weighed against the rest of the canonical witness? Some texts in the Bible are deeply and undeniably problematic, of course, and should not be equated in any facile ways with the will of God.

From a more historical-critical perspective, how did the parable—in whole and in part—form Matthean communities of faith for their participation within the larger purposes of God? And in what ways might it continue to form our own contemporary communities for missional participation today? In what ways does Matt 18:21–35 confirm and underscore our assumptions about the good news of what God is purposefully doing, and how does it challenge and expand our perspectives? How does it reorient

---

In a similar vein, Johnson notes how metaphorical language for God can be helpful as long as we continue to recognize and acknowledge "the active tension between similarity and dissimilarity, between the 'is' and the 'is not' of the two terms" (19). The problem is that "religious tradition with its habitual repetition in ritual and teaching is liable to forget this pivotal point. But without the tension of 'is and is not,' metaphors get taken literally and become trite, losing their power to shock and surprise" (20).

As authors, we come to the table with theological commitments and denominational affiliations, but we must always hold those things with lightness and humility in the face of divine ineffability. Our convictions and various traditions concerning God are not God. While we write out of traditions with robust creedal frameworks, we seek to take seriously the fact that these pointers to God are not themselves God. The liberative missional hermeneutics we are proposing seeks to embody and enact the humility, circumspection, and incompleteness that analogy and metaphor necessitate.

us away from our cultural assumptions and calculative tendencies, toward a different set of *missional* considerations?

Of course, Matt 18:21–35 is but one text within the entire biblical canon that can and should be explored missionally. Again, the missional posture toward biblical interpretation that we are advocating is an approach that can be applied to *all* of Scripture, to *any* biblical text. To be sure, not all texts will be equally revelatory of divine purposes or the faith community's participation within them—and, indeed, many individual pericopes, taken on their own, will undoubtedly seem to run *against* the grain of divine purposes. In any event, as we have already noted, it is critical that we recognize that missional hermeneutics is not about finding something specific in the Bible about or even related to mission, traditionally understood, but rather that we need to come to everything in the Bible asking missionally located questions about what it contains and what it may communicate to readers. Inasmuch as the biblical canon, in whole and in part, is a product of and tool for the formation of reading communities such that they may participate faithfully in the larger purposes of God, every text in Scripture needs to be approached *missionally* so as to read it on its own terms, whether or not it has anything to do with evangelism or other forms of traditional missionary outreach.

Missional Engagement with Gen 38 and Lev 25

Let us briefly consider two other examples of texts—now from the Old Testament—that may help underscore again how different missional interpretation is from traditional attempts to find "mission texts" in the Bible. Again, remember that previous generations of interpreters often failed to find much evidence of mission in the Old Testament, precisely because they defined mission narrowly in terms of cross-cultural outreach and evangelism.

First, we turn to Gen 38:1–30, which is decidedly *not* a traditional "mission text," having nothing to say about evangelism and outreach. And, even from the more holistic perspective of missional hermeneutics, it would be misguided and foolish to imagine that every detail in the infamous story of Judah and Tamar—replete with divinely orchestrated deaths and sexually troubling scenarios, including incest—could reveal unvarnished insights into divine purposiveness. Nevertheless, Judah's final assessment of his interactions with Tamar—"She is more in the right than I" (38:26)—particularly in view of the way he had economically mistreated his daughter-in-law, has significant missional implications for reading communities, even today, in radically different sociocultural contexts.

Contemporary Christians may be understandably scandalized by the salacious and off-putting sexual dynamics in the story (see, in this regard, the passage in Deut 25:5–10 outlining levirate marriage). But Judah's last statement in v. 26 makes it clear that, from a biblical vantage point, unjust economic treatment of the vulnerable by the powerful may even be worse than some highly problematic "bedroom" behaviors that may tend more regularly to catch our attention today.

As with many passages across the biblical canon, Gen 38 suggests that enacting justice for the economically vulnerable (and specifically for widows like Tamar [e.g., Exod 22:22–24; Deut 10:16–19; 27:19; cf. Jas 1:27]) is more of a divine priority than we may often recognize or acknowledge. The story of Tamar and Judah has much for contemporary communities of faith to reflect on, particularly as we seek to participate faithfully within the *missio Dei*. While it is not a *traditional* mission text, it can be read fruitfully with a missional posture. And the passage clearly has something to say about Tamar's liberation—in concrete, economic terms. Indeed, in this sense, her vindication and liberation seem to be primary concerns of the text. At the same time, there can be little doubt that Judah, too, is at the threshold of experiencing a kind of liberation himself, even if previously he had betrayed no awareness of his need for it. In reckoning with and acknowledging his own unjust behavior toward Tamar, he too can begin to step into a new future. Perhaps we're not as far removed from these stories as we might at first imagine.

Ultimately, the narrative provides critical formation for contemporary communities of faith today—and in every subsequent age. Genesis 38 is a bracing reminder that economic exploitation was and is a matter of deep missional concern for God. Economic justice and the liberation it provides for all involved—both oppressor and oppressed—must remain an abiding concern for today's missional communities lest we find ourselves participating more in Judah's unrighteousness than within divine purposes.

Second, let us reflect briefly on the year of Jubilee in Lev 25, one of the most obviously and emphatically liberative texts in the Bible—and a passage that has not received the attention it deserves from most Christians in North America.[7] The biblical scenario is as follows: in Israel, all debts

7. For additional discussion of the Jubilee that informs our comments here, please see

were to be forgiven—wiped clean—every seventh year. Concurrently, agricultural lands were to lay fallow, enabling the soil to be replenished and providing clear opportunities for God's people to practice trust in divine provision for food. (There is a clear connection between the rest and restorative rhythm provided during the weekly sabbath and this seventh-year sabbatical.) As loans were directly related to human need, they were not to become tools for economic exploitation and enslavement. (Not insignificantly, lenders were prohibited from charging any interest on loans, given that those seeking loans were overwhelmingly from among the poor.) Regular, iterative cancelation of debts, reflecting divine priorities and purposes, functioned to keep human need rather than profit-seeking at the forefront of social considerations. The poor, liberated from indebtedness every seventh year, were enabled to begin afresh. Past challenges were not to inhibit present and future possibilities.

The Jubilee legislation in Lev 25 goes even further. Every seventh cycle of seven years—that is, every fiftieth year—all debts were again to be cancelled, even as agricultural land remained fallow. In addition, all rural landholdings were to be returned to their original owners. In effect, this "sabbath of Sabbaths" every fiftieth year ensured that those experiencing economic difficulty would not become endlessly mired in transgenerational poverty. Since land was the primary and most important form of economic capital in the ancient world, the Jubilee provided perpetual means of liberation for the poor, as God—the true owner of all land—took up their cause by requiring its regular redistribution.

Note that the Jubilee provisions were not predicated on—or even related to—any generosity or philanthropic impulse on the part of wealthy members of the community. As a regularized, divinely sanctioned structural mechanism for what amounted to massive societal wealth redistribution, the Jubilee was rooted in divine justice rather than human charity. Moreover, the legislation placed the onus for change not upon the poor—as is so often the case in capitalistic conversations about poverty and inequality—but rather on those who were already well resourced. Leviticus 25 required that those with land not included in their original ancestral holdings return it to those who, for whatever reason, had lost access to it during the preceding fifty-year cycle.

Barram, "Economic and Social Reparations"; for an expanded version of that essay, see "Reparational Reasoning"; see also Barram, *Missional Economics*, 111–19.

While much more could be said about the Jubilee, suffice it to say that Lev 25 provides significant insight into God's character and purposes. The God of the Jubilee is a God of justice who provides for the meeting of all human need. Land and all resources that support human life and flourishing belong to and are provided by God, in trust. God provides abundance even as we humans continually resort to behaviors rooted in our assumptions of scarcity. The good news is that God remains attentive to the needs of those who are vulnerable and marginalized. Indeed, such attentiveness is a core facet of who God is and what God is up to (see, e.g., Deut 10:12–22). And God's liberative action on behalf of the poor has, in fact, liberative effects even for the non-poor: when some suffer, all are dehumanized to some degree in the process of attempting to maintain a dehumanizing system. When the oppressed are liberated, everyone—including oppressors—have the opportunity to experience greater personhood and freedom.

Strikingly, this is precisely what Zacchaeus discovers in Luke's Gospel (19:1–10) when he is found and truly seen by Jesus. Sharing a meal with the messiah, Zacchaeus promises to atone for and repair any damage he has inflicted upon others: "Look, half of my possessions, Lord, I will give to the poor; and if I have defrauded anyone of anything, I will pay back four times as much" (v. 8).[8] The tax collector commits himself to enact a form of Jubilee-style wealth redistribution, promising, in effect, to make *reparations* for past injustices.[9] While his actions will undoubtedly have liberative consequences for those to whom he will make amends, we must not overlook the fact that Jesus announces the arrival of Zacchaeus's "salvation" *in response to* the tax collector's promise to repair the damage he has caused. Biblically, economic justice and salvation are regularly connected (cf. Matt 25:31–46; Mark 10:17–31; Luke 16:19–31). Divine liberation is a many-splendored phenomenon, and we are missionally called to participate in that liberative activity.

Recall that Jesus inaugurates his own mission in Luke 4 by reading from Isaiah. Neither the prophet nor Jesus conceive of divine purposes in terms that privilege purely "spiritual" matters over physical and material concerns:

---

8. This reading of v. 8 reflects the NRSV. Another possible reading, given the present-tense Greek verbs in v. 8, would be to understand Zacchaeus as already doing these things; Jesus's response in v. 9 would serve to announce his righteousness before his opponents.

9. On the Jubilee and reparations, including Zacchaeus, see Kwon and Thompson, *Reparations*; Barram, "Reparational Reasoning"; see also Rhodes, "From Here to Jubilee."

The Spirit of the Lord is upon me,
  because he has anointed me
  to bring good news to the poor.
He has sent me to proclaim release to the captives
  and recovery of sight to the blind,
    to let the oppressed go free,
  to proclaim the year of the Lord's favor. (Luke 4:18–19)

Indeed, scholars widely recognize that the last line, with its reference to "the year of the Lord's favor" (v. 19), invokes nothing less than the year of Jubilee itself. If Jesus understands the reading from Isaiah as an adequate summary of his own purposes (v. 21: "Today this scripture has been fulfilled in your hearing"), we would be hard pressed not to see our own understanding of the church's mission in similar terms.

Reading Missionally for Liberation

It bears repeating: missional hermeneutics endeavors to approach biblical texts in ways that liberate them to speak about God and God's people in ways that are consonant with the missional character of the texts themselves. We ask not *Is there mission in this text?* but rather *How and what does this particular text reveal about the missio Dei and faithful human participation within it?* That question applies to biblical passages regardless of genre, across both testaments. Some texts may reveal much; others may not. But every text, in any genre, can be explored from a missional posture.

Some scriptural passages readily and quite obviously lend themselves to missional interpretation. For example, prophetic texts, Wisdom Literature, and many of the New Testament letters are explicit in trying to shape communal behavior such that faith communities can and will begin to participate more faithfully in divine purposes. Likewise, the creation narratives, significant portions of the Pentateuchal law codes, biblical poetry, the Gospels and Acts, and even apocalyptic literature often seek to illuminate divine intentionality—and human vocation in relation to the *missio Dei*—quite clearly and explicitly. We may approach each of these texts with missionally located questions, cognizant and respectful of their various genres and subgenres, asking what and how they contribute to and expand our understandings of what God is up to and how we are being called to participate.

Some passages, given their specific characteristics, will prove resistant—or at least they may not seem as readily accessible or appropriate as others—with regard to divine purposiveness or human participation. Perhaps the most challenging texts to read missionally, particularly in the explicitly liberative manner we are proposing here, will be those that prove difficult and off-putting no matter how we read them today—such as passages that advocate violence, condone slavery, or foster misogyny and undergird patriarchy. It can be unsettling to discover that ancient biblical authors and editors regularly described their sociocultural perspectives and conduct as being divinely authorized or explicitly commanded by God. It is the Bible, after all. Nevertheless, it's true: parochial animosities and violence against political rivals were often framed as rooted in divine initiative. And hierarchies rooted in traditional assumptions about gender, sexual norms, and the ubiquity of slavery were either taken for granted or understood to be divinely sanctioned.

A liberative missional hermeneutics does not shrink from such passages, but neither does it approach them uncritically or with naïve deference to the ways in which they have been traditionally interpreted. In such cases, we suggest that interpreters must be willing to read against the grain of texts, trusting in the wisdom of the Spirit—and perhaps even reject the apparent implications of certain passages. That is because some biblical texts seem to betray their human cultural contexts more than they offer clear and unobstructed windows into divine purposefulness. This is always a challenging dynamic. While we must not simply accept what we like and reject what we do not, we need to recognize and come to terms with the fact that God's word in Scripture always comes to us through creaturely and cultural refraction.

Communication—even biblical communication—is necessarily incomplete. We must continually try not to mistake the culturally incidental for that which is divinely purposeful and enduring, exchanging what is limited and peripheral for what is abundant and central. This is neither easy nor a one-time activity. We read in community with the Spirit's guidance. Disagreements are to be anticipated, but as Jesus's followers we commit to struggling and discerning together in love. Love, mercy, and justice—all key to complete liberation and intrinsic to the biblical canon—can serve as reliable and useful interpretive guidance as we seek discern and participate with divine purposes.

Indeed, lest those of us who seek theological precision and who comfort ourselves with adherence to narrow orthodoxies forget, Scripture is clear that love is the key to everything, including interpretation. This is such a pivotal matter that it merits brief but explicit reference to—and deep meditation upon—a few seminal texts. As Jesus himself indicates, two statements from Torah—from Deut 6:5 and Lev 19:18, respectively, sum up all that matters:

> "You shall love the Lord your God with all your heart, and with all your soul, and with all your mind." This is the greatest and first commandment. And a second is like it: "You shall love your neighbor as yourself. On these two commandments hang all the law and the prophets." (Matt 22:37–40)

Even a self-justifying expert in Torah understood as much, even though Jesus had to help him live more fully into the implications of loving God and neighbor (through the parable of the loving Samaritan; Luke 10:25–37). And in his letter to the Roman Christians, Paul echoes a similar point, focusing directly on the second of the two commands:

> Owe no one anything, except to love one another; for the one who loves another has fulfilled the law. The commandments, "You shall not commit adultery; You shall not murder; You shall not steal; You shall not covet"; and any other commandment, are summed up in this word, "Love your neighbor as yourself. Love does no wrong to a neighbor; therefore, love is the fulfilling of the law." (Rom 13:8–10)

Perhaps most striking of all are the apostle's powerful words to Jesus's disjointed community in Corinth:

> If I speak in the tongues of mortals and of angels, but do not have love, I am a noisy gong or a clanging cymbal. And if I have prophetic powers, and understand all mysteries and all knowledge, and if I have all faith, so as to remove mountains, but do not have love, I am nothing. If I give away all my possessions, and if I hand over my body so that I may boast, but do not have love, I gain nothing. (1 Cor 13:1–3)

Without love, we have nothing. Therefore, to affirm love as an interpretive guide for interpreting Scripture is not some kind of theologically wishy-washy, progressive cop out. On the contrary, love is the point, and this is especially true of a liberative missional hermeneutics. As 1 John 4 argues, "whoever does not love does not know God, for God is love" (v. 8). That same author insists that "God is love, and those who abide in love abide in God, and God abides in them" (v. 16). Biblically speaking, love is who God is, what God cares about, and what God is up to. Since our mission is always derivative of God's, we must understand our participation in divine purposes in precisely those terms. And this means that we should proceed with great caution before we choose to discern the character and purposes of God in Scripture through an interpretive perspective other than love.

Ultimately, the Bible illuminates God's loving character and purposes as well as the nature and role of the faith community called to participate in those purposes. To focus on those matters as we interpret the Bible is to begin to read it *missionally*. Doing so serves to liberate both Scripture and us by opening us up to infinite mystery and possibility. Such liberation can help to foster more authentic, engaged, and faithful participation in what God is purposefully—*missionally*—doing in the world. Again, in every case, missional hermeneutics involves asking questions that seek to illuminate divine purposes and our own participation within them. Naturally, therefore, the missional questions we might ask of any given biblical text are potentially endless. The answers to such questions are never for us merely matters of "theology" or "belief" or even "ethics." They will press toward more engaged, faithful, and life-giving *participation* in the liberating mission of God.[10]

Participating in Missional Hermeneutics: Getting Started

While we believe that it is important for readers to understand some of the basics of missional hermeneutics—and some of the nuances involved—a key goal for us in writing this book has been to help others begin to *participate* in this kind of interpretative posture. We recognize that much of the foregoing discussion of missional hermeneutics, while informative, may still leave some readers wondering *how, specifically*, to begin engaging biblical texts missionally. So, we conclude with a brief *how to* framework that can be easily and readily incorporated into personal or group studies. What follows are a number of questions, grouped broadly around the three lenses of interpretation that we have examined, which we hope can help readers and interpreters begin to participate fruitfully in missional

10. For a thoughtful and helpful exploration of these issues, see McKenzie, "Hermeneutics of Participation."

interpretation. We offer these questions as a useful starting point for you and your communities as you seek to engage biblical texts from a missional posture. While these questions need not be addressed in an exhaustive way or in any precise order, we suggest that exploring them in something like the arrangement given below should prove, through the Spirit's guidance, to be profoundly liberating—both for Scripture itself and for those of us who read it for missional participation in divine purposes.

1. Coming to the Text as Missionally Located Readers (in front of the text)

   • What "locations" do we come from as readers, personally and collectively, and how may those locational dynamics affect how we read this text and what we will be able to see and hear in it?

   • Within what contextual context/s (historically, socioculturally, politically, economically, etc.) are we reading this text? How, specifically, are we as readers "missionally located" in this particular confluence of contexts?

   • What is happening "on the ground," as it were, in the locations where we might typically read this text? What role do those locational dynamics play in what we might find ourselves looking for in this text? How might they affect how we interpret what we find in this text?

2. Exploring God's Mission (in the text itself)

   • What might this text communicate about God's purposes, and how does it do so?

   • How might this text reflect, contribute to, and/or complexify a/the larger (e.g., canonical) story of divine purposiveness?

   • What does this text say (or imply) about who God is?

   • What does this text say (or imply) about what God cares about?

   • What does this text say (or imply) about what God is up to?

   • (That is, what does this text say [or imply] about divine purposes?)

   • How, and in what way/s does this text seem to fit into, reflect, and further the larger story of God's purposes as we find them across the biblical canon? That is, what role or function does this text seem to play within the larger biblical story of God's mission?

3. **Human Participation in God's Mission (in the text itself)**

- What might this text communicate about human participation in God's purposes, and how does it do so?

- How might this text reflect, contribute to, and/or complexify a/ the larger (e.g., canonical) story of human participation in divine purposes?

- What does this text say (or imply) about human beings in relation to who God is?

- What does this text say (or imply) about human beings in relation to what God cares about?

- What does this text say (or imply) about human beings in relation to what God is up to?

- How, and in what way/s does this text seem to fit into, reflect, and further the larger story of human participation within God's purposes as we find them across the biblical canon? That is, what role or function does this text seem to play within the larger biblical story of the mission of God's people?

4. **Formation for Participation in God's Mission (behind and in front of the text)**

- In what way/s do the authors/editors of this text seem to have sought (through this text) to form, shape, and equip their original readers for their participation in God's purposes?

- How, and in what way/s might this text have effectively formed, shaped, and equipped its original readers for their participation in God's purposes?

- How, and in what way/s might this text continue to form, shape, and equip its readers today, given the very different contexts in which they are located as participants in God's mission?

- What does reading this text with a missional posture reveal about us and about how we have been interpreting and using Scripture?

- In what ways have we been shaped by the contextual frameworks within which we are embedded more than we are shaped by Scripture?

What have our mythologies and ideologies led us to miss, or to misrepresent, about divine purposes?

- How does the text both illuminate and challenge the assumptions and norms of our contextual locatedness?

- How might this text—and our reading of it—contribute to or inhibit the decolonization of the Christian assumptions, beliefs, institutions, and practices? In what ways does this text challenge us to recognize the power dynamics within which we read and live our lives?

- Does our interpretation of the text resonate with those who have often found themselves on the "underside" of power structures? Is the agency of the vulnerable and voiceless enhanced or undermined by our reading? Does our reading reinforce power inequities characteristic of colonizing systems in which the vulnerable many are exploited for the benefit of the powerful few?

- How might this text—and our reading of it—contribute to or inhibit the liberating work that Scripture is to have within the lives and communities of its readers? Is there good news in this text for communities of faith that are gathered around it—and what are the missional implications of that news for those communities who are called to embody it?

- What might happen to our understanding of God's purposes—and our participation within them—as we read this text with others who come to it from different "locations"?

In addition to these questions, we also suggest consideration of those that were highlighted in chapter 2, which we include again here. (Remember that these are merely illustrative questions to help our readers get started on the road of missional reflection and interpretation.)

- How does our reading of a given text demonstrate humility—recognizing that we see and understand only in part?

- Does our reading of the text challenge or baptize our assumptions and blind spots? In what ways are we tempted to "spiritualize" the concrete implications of the gospel as articulated in this text?

- How does the text help to clarify appropriate Christian behavior—not only in terms of conduct but also in terms of intentionality and motive?

- Does our reading emphasize the triumph of Christ's resurrection to the exclusion of the kenotic, cruciform character of his ministry?

- In what ways does this text proclaim good news to the poor and release to the captives, and how might our own social locations make it difficult to hear that news as good?

- Does our reading of the text reflect a tendency to bifurcate evangelism and justice?

- Does our reading of this text acknowledge and confess our complicity and culpability in personal as well as structural sin?

- In what ways does the text challenge us to rethink our often-cozy relationships with power and privilege?

- How does this text expose and challenge our societal and economic tendencies to assign human beings and the rest of creation merely functional, as opposed to inherent, value?

- Does the text help clarify the call of gospel discipleship in a world of conspicuous consumption, devastating famine, rampant disease, incessant war, and vast economic inequities?

- How does the text clarify what love of God and neighbor looks like in a particular context?

- How does this text clarify what God is doing in our world, in our nation, in our cities, and in our neighborhoods—and how may we be called to be involved in those purposes?

- Does our reading allow the text the opportunity to define everything about our mission in the world—including our assumptions, processes, terminology—everything?

Toward Liberative Participation

As we have repeatedly indicated, missional hermeneutics does not provide singularly definitive readings of Scripture; rather, this approach to biblical interpretation foregrounds the kinds of questions and considerations that can and should be in view when engaging any scriptural passage. A missional posture neither dictates from the outset what the results of textual analysis will be, nor necessitates any once-for-all-times-and-contexts conclusions.

From our perspective, though, this does not mean that any and all purportedly "missional" readings of Scripture are of equal value and import.

We have come to believe that missional hermeneutics can and should help to liberate biblical texts from our attempts, inadvertent or otherwise, to control and tame them—even as it encourages and fosters cooperation with the Spirit's work in liberating and forming us through Scripture for faithful and joyful participation in what the purposeful God of the Bible is up to. Ultimately, we would argue that missional readings of biblical texts must be liberative at some level and in some way. A liberative element—even when surprising or counterintuitive—should differentiate missional hermeneutics, as we envision it, from any interpretive approaches that foster dynamics such as judgmentalism, dehumanization, retribution, and control instead of attunement to divine love, mercy, justice, and liberation. What this means will, of course, differ in varying contexts. But a reading that fails to reflect something of the liberative love that the God of the Bible intends for humanity and, indeed, for all of creation, should remain especially suspect. The logic here is relatively straightforward: God's mission involves bringing about a new kind of reality, a completely upsidedown kind of empire—what Jesus called the reign of God—a rule that would be nothing short of the complete embodiment of utterly good news. Ultimately, we submit, missional hermeneutics is characterized by a posture of interpretive participation in that liberative, purposive movement of God. May Scripture be increasingly liberated from our well-intended but problematic assumptions and perspectives, even as it helps to foster our own liberation—and the liberation of all of creation!

Afterword

By Lisa Bowens

Princeton Theological Seminary

Liberating. Liberative missional hermeneutics. Missional hermeneutics of liberating love.

FOR SOME INTERPRETERS WHO think about or have heard about missional hermeneutics, the above descriptors do not cohere to their conception of missional interpretation. For these interpreters, the terms mission and missional hermeneutics denote anything but liberation and love. Due to historical tragedies and traumas wrought by missionaries and missionary movements, and the ongoing legacies of those tragedies and traumas, some are quite suspicious of the missional interpretive framework. Yet these descriptors, all of which appear in this book, *Liberating Scripture*, signify Michael Barram's and John Franke's aim to reframe the missional hermeneutics discourse. But is such a reframing possible in light of history?

In 1949 in his book *Jesus and the Disinherited*, renowned theologian and preacher Howard Thurman wrote about the cooptation of Christianity by the powerful and the dominant, including the cooptation of the missionary project. He writes, "It is the sin of pride and arrogance that has tended to vitiate the missionary impulse and to make of it an instrument of self-righteousness on the one hand and racial superiority on the other."[1]

---

1. Thurman, *Jesus and the Disinherited*, 2–3.

For Thurman, the missionary impulse that is so much a part of Christian thought is problematic because it facilitates dominance and self-importance. Historically, many of those engaged in mission saw themselves as superior to those they helped. Again, Thurman: "For decades we have studied the various peoples of the world and those who live as our neighbors as objects of missionary endeavor and enterprise without being at all willing to treat them either as brothers or as human beings."[2]

In *Liberating Scripture*, Barram and Franke attempt not only to liberate scripture but also to liberate missional hermeneutics and unshackle it from the ways in which the concept of the *missio Dei* has been misused as chronicled by Thurman. The "missionary impulse" has led to the oppression, colonization, and dehumanization of many nonwhite peoples around the world. Both Barram and Franke, leading scholars in the current missional hermeneutics conversation, recognize and give voice to this troubled history in the preceding pages. In addition, they are intentional about the need to separate the notion of evangelistic outreach/mission, which is prominent in some circles, from the missional hermeneutics project. The two are not the same.

Accordingly, Barram and Franke remain committed to reframing and recalibrating missional hermeneutics by offering a particular vision for this interpretive enterprise, a vision that is inclusive and provocative, with the potential for stimulating new conversations about the meaning and relevance of biblical interpretation in the twenty-first century. With an emphasis on listening to the marginalized, the other, the oppressed, and their interpretations of scripture, the project Barram and Franke propose in this monograph provides a possible way forward for rethinking what missional hermeneutics should be about and what it should actually entail. Missional hermeneutics should not be about dominating or colonizing people or expanding the goals of empire. No longer are people objects at whom mission is directed but subjects who discern what God is up to in the world and who join in God's liberative project.[3] Moreover, the idea put forward in this volume, that the *missio Dei* is about the purposes of God and centers around three questions: Who is God? What does God care about? And what is God up to?, has the potential to reinvigorate the missional conversation and its intersection with biblical exegesis.

2. Thurman, *Jesus and the Disinherited*, 3.

3. This language of discerning and joining in derives from Michael Gorman, whose work Barram and Franke discuss in this book. See Gorman, *Becoming the Gospel*, 53.

In view of such questions, what would it mean to reimagine the *missio Dei* in light of how many early black exegetes of the eighteenth and nineteenth centuries understood God? In this time period, considered by some as one of the high points of the mission movement, a number of black interpreters countered one of the dominant views of God at the time: God as one who sanctions and ordains black enslavement. If one were to pose the question, "Who is God?," to significant African American figures of this period, such as Lemuel Haynes, Zilpha Elaw, and James Pennington, one of the answers they would probably give is that God is a liberator and a deliverer. What happens when we envision missional theology in that way or start with that understanding of a missional hermeneutic? The mission that God is up to and what God cares about is the mission of liberation. God is liberating, delivering, and rescuing and so we are called to participate in God's liberating project. This liberating project involves freeing individuals as well as communities, nations, and the world from destructive powers and forces; this divine liberation is wholistic, incorporating scripture itself as demonstrated in the preceding pages.

Both Barram and Franke extend an invitation to readers to reimagine, rethink, re-engage, and reignite the missional hermeneutics conversation. This book may well serve as the spark needed for such a dialogue.

The Forum on Missional Hermeneutics: Session History

2002 Breakfast meeting keynote

James V. Brownson, Western Theological Seminary
"An Adequate Missional Hermeneutic"

2003 Breakfast meeting keynote

Michael Barram, Saint Mary's College of California
"Toward a Missiological Hermeneutic: The Bible and Mission in Current and Future Discussion"

2004 Breakfast meeting keynote

Grant LeMarquand, Trinity Episcopal School for Ministry
"From Creation to New Creation: The Mission of God in the Biblical Story"

2005 Paper Session

Christopher J. H. Wright, Langham Partnership International
"Making Missional Sense of the Old Testament: Does It Work?"

Respondent: James V. Brownson, Western Theological Seminary

Colin Yuckman, United Presbyterian Church of New Kensington (PA)
"An Ulterior Gospel: The Mission of Critical Hermeneutics and the Critical Hermeneutics of Mission"

Respondent: Michael Barram, Saint Mary's College of California

James Miller, Asbury Theological Seminary
"Missional Hermeneutics: An Experiment in Implementation and Reflection"

Respondent: Grant LeMarquand, Trinity School of Ministry

2006 Paper Session

Presider: George Hunsberger, Western Theological Seminary

Michael Goheen, Trinity Western University
"Notes toward a Framework for a Missional Hermeneutic"

Michael Barram, Saint Mary's College of California
"'Located Questions' for a Missional Hermeneutic"

2007 Theme—Missional Hermeneutics in the Classroom: Philippians

Darrell Guder, Princeton Theological Seminary
J. Ross Wagner, Princeton Theological Seminary
Joint presentation on teaching a missional reading of Philippians at Princeton Theological Seminary

2008 Theme—Mapping the Missional Hermeneutics Conversation

Paper presentation (given twice, first at the American Academy of Religion meetings; then at the Society of Biblical Literature meetings)

George R. Hunsberger, Western Theological Seminary
"Proposals for a Missional Hermeneutic: Mapping a
Conversation"

Respondent (at AAR): Michael Barram, Saint Mary's College
of California

Respondent (at SBL): James V. Brownson, Western Theological
Seminary

2009 Theme: "Missional Readings of Paul's Letter to the Philippians"
Presider: George R. Hunsberger, Western Theological Seminary

Michael Barram, Saint Mary's College of California
"Reflections on the Practice of Missional Hermeneutics:
'Streaming' Philippians 1:20–30"

James C. Miller, Asbury Theological Seminary
"Missionally Mapping Philippians"

Michael J. Gorman, Saint Mary's Seminary and University
"The Apologetic and Missional Impulse of Philippians 2:6–11
in the Context of the Letter"

Respondent: Stephen E. Fowl, Loyola College in Maryland

2010 Theme: "Exile, Identity, and Mission: Interpreting Biblical Texts"
Paper session (call for papers)

Presider: Michael Barram, Saint Mary's College of California

Bo Lim, Seattle Pacific University
"From Servant to Servants: Continuing the Legacy of the Exile in
the Post Exilic Era"

Andy Rowell, Duke Divinity School
"John Howard Yoder's Missional Exiles and Jeremiah 29: A Case
Study for Missional Hermeneutics"

Aaron Kuecker, Trinity Christian College
"As He Who Called You Is Holy: Missional Holiness
and the People of God in 1 Peter"

Respondent: George R. Hunsberger, Western Theological Seminary

Respondent: Suzanne Watts Henderson, Queen's University
of Charlotte

2011 Session 1—Theme: "Reading the Parables of Jesus Missionally"
Presider: George R. Hunsberger, Western Theological Seminary

Jason S. Sexton, University of St. Andrews
"Reading the Parables Theologically to Read Them Missionally:
A Missional Reading of the Early Galilean Parables in Luke's
Gospel"

Lois Barrett, Associated Mennonite Biblical Seminary
"Reading Matthew 13 Missionally: Training for
the Reign of God"

Colin H. Yuckman, United Presbyterian Church of New Kensington
"A Shadow of a Magnitude: Reading Luke's 'Parables of the Lost'
Missionally"

Respondent: Klyne Snodgrass, North Park University

2011 Session 2—Theme: "Panel Discussion of Michael J. Gorman's
*Reading Revelation Responsibly: Uncivil Worship and Witness:
Following the Lamb into the New Creation"* (Cascade, 2011)
Presider: Michael Barram, Saint Mary's College of California

Panelists: Darrell Guder, Princeton Theological Seminary
John R. Franke, First Presbyterian Church, Allentown, PA
James V. Brownson, Western Theological Seminary
Sylvia Keesmaat, Trinity College in the University of Toronto

Respondent: Michael J. Gorman, Saint Mary's Seminary and
University

2012 Session 1—Theme: "Review Panel Discussion of C. Kavin Rowe's
World Upside Down: Reading Acts in the Graeco-Roman Age"
(Oxford University Press, 2009)

Presider: George R. Hunberger, Western Theological Seminary

Panelists: C. Kavin Rowe, Duke University
Dennis Edwards, Saint Mary's Seminary and University
Christina Busman, Bethel University
James C. Miller, Asbury Theological Seminary
Colin Yuckman, United Presbyterian Church of New Kensington
(PA)

Respondent: C. Kavin Rowe, Duke University

2012 Session 2—Theme: "Reading Genesis 1–11 Missionally"

Presider: Lois Barrett, Associated Mennonite Biblical Seminary

Luke Ben Tallon, Pepperdine University
  "Is There Any There There? Genesis 1–3 as a Prophetic Call
  for Truly Local Churches"

Michael Barram, Saint Mary's College of California
  "'Occupying' Genesis 1–3: Missionally Located Reflections
  on Biblical Economic Values and Justice"

James K. Mead, Northwestern College (Iowa)
  "Cast the Ark upon the Waters: A Missional Reading
  of the Flood Story"

Respondent: Christopher J. H. Wright, Langham Partnership International

2013 Session 1—Theme: "The Corinthian Correspondence and Missional Praxis"

Presider: Eunice McGarrahan, First Presbyterian Church, Colorado Springs

Michael Barram, Saint Mary's College of California
   "'Fools for the Sake of Christ': Missional Hermeneutics and Praxis in the Corinthian Correspondence"

Andy Rowell, Duke Divinity School
   "The Missional Ecclesiology of First Corinthians 14"

Dustin Ellington, Justo Mwale Theological University College, Lusaka, Zambia
   "Corinthian Transformation for Mission: Re-Interpreting 2 Corinthians 4"

Matthew Forrest Lowe, Lectio House, Ontario
   "'Although We Live in the World . . .': The Mission of God and the Mission of Empire in 2 Corinthians 10"

Respondent: Richard B. Hays, Duke Divinity School

2013 Session 2—Theme: "Assessing and Advancing Missional Hermeneutics"

Presider: Christina Busman, Bethel University

George R. Hunsberger, Western Theological Seminary
   "Convictions Formed and Futures Waiting: A Traveler's Response to the Journey thus Far"

John R. Franke, Yellowstone Theological Institute
"Treasures Old and New: Considerations on the Future
of Missional Hermeneutics"

2014 Session 1—Theme: "Thinking Missionally about God, Scripture, and Missional Vocation"

Presider: Jeff Greenman, Regent College

Derek Taylor, Duke University
"Is Israel a Missionary Failure? Isaiah's Servant of Yahweh
and a New Telling of the Missio Dei"

James C. Miller, Asbury Theological Seminary
"Suffering as a Component of the Mission of God"

Kelly Liebengood, LeTourneau University
"Participating in the Life of the Triune God: Reconsidering
the Trinitarian Foundation of 1 Peter's Missional Identity"

Respondent: Darrell L. Guder, Princeton Theological Seminary

Respondent: George Hunsberger, Western Theological Seminary

2014 Session 2—Theme: "Reflecting on Paul and Missional Hermeneutics: A Conversation with N. T. Wright"

Presiding: John Franke, Yellowstone Theological Institute

Panelists: N. T. Wright, University of St. Andrews
Sylvia Keesmaat, Toronto School of Theology
Michael J. Gorman, Saint Mary's Seminary and University
James V. Brownson, Western Theological Seminary

Respondent: N. T. Wright, University of St. Andrews

2014 Session 3—Theme: "Thinking Missionally about God, Scripture, and Missional Vocation"

Presider: Lois Barrett, Anabaptist Mennonite Biblical Seminary

Andy Johnson, Nazarene Theological Seminary
"Ecclesiology, Election, and Holiness: A Missional Reading of the Thessalonian Correspondence"

Colin H. Yuckman, Duke Divinity School
"'That the Works of God Should Be Made Manifest': Vision and Vocation in John 9"

Respondent: Eunice McGarrahan, First Presbyterian Church, Colorado Springs

Respondent: Michael Barram, Saint Mary's College of California

2015 Session 1—Theme: "Biblical Formation of the Congregation for Missional Witness"

Presider: James C. Miller, Asbury Theological Seminary

Mark Glanville, Trinity College—University of Bristol
"Radical Gratitude and the Mission of God: Nourishing Celebration and Inclusivism in Local Congregations in Light of the Festival Calendar, Deuteronomy 16:1–17"

Boaz Johnson, North Park University
"Missional Theology and Congregation Formation in the Torah"

Michael Barram, Saint Mary's College of California
"To Serve God and Not Mammon: Reading Matthew 6 as Missionally Located Formation for Economic Discipleship"

Respondent: Mark Labberton, Fuller Theological Seminary

2015 Session 2—Theme: "Review Panel Discussion of Michael J. Gorman's *Becoming the Gospel: Paul, Participation, and Mission*" (Eerdmans, 2015)

Presider: Sylvia Keesmaat, Trinity College, University of Toronto

Panelists: Michael J. Gorman, Saint Mary's Seminary and University
J. Ross Wagner, Duke Divinity School
Eunice McGarrahan, First Presbyterian Church, Colorado Springs
George R. Hunsberger, Western Theological Seminary
John R. Franke, Evangelische Theologische Faculteit, Leuven

Respondent: Michael J. Gorman, Saint Mary's Seminary and University

2015 Session 3—Theme: "Biblical Formation of the Congregation for Missional Witness"

Presider: Darrell L. Guder, Princeton Theological Seminary

Laura R. Levens, Baptist Seminary of Kentucky
"Many Voices, Many Contexts, One Faith: Engaging the Breadth of Scripture to Form Discerning, Missional Congregations"

Luke Ben Tallon and Aaron Kuecker, LeTourneau University
"A Liturgy of Ascent and a Life of Ascent: Conforming Congregations to Christian Scripture"

Derek W. Taylor, Duke University
"Forming Faithful Readers: Dietrich Bonhoeffer's Missional Hermeneutic"

Respondent: Benjamin T. Conner, Western Theological Seminary

2016 Session 1—Theme: "Migration, Marginalization, and the Mission of God: Missional Hermeneutics in the Context of Human Displacement and Relocation"

Presider: George Hunsberger, Western Theological Seminary

Mark Glanville, Trinity College, Bristol
  "Family for the Displaced: A Missional Reading
  of Deuteronomy 10:17–19"

Helen Taylor Boursier, University of Saint Mary, Leavenworth, KS
  "Faithful Doxology: Deuteronomy 16:18–20 and the Church's
  Missional Participation with Immigrants Seeking Asylum"

Respondent: Michael Barram, Saint Mary's College of California

2016 Session 2—A Discussion of the Argument and Impact—After Nearly Twenty Years—of *Speaking the Truth in Love: New Testament Resources for a Missional Hermeneutic* (Trinity Press, 1998), by James V. Brownson

Presiding: John Franke, Second Presbyterian Church, Indianapolis

Panelists: James Brownson, Western Theological Seminary
Megan DeFranza, Boston University
Daniel Lee, Fuller Theological Seminary
Drew Hart, Messiah College
David Congdon, InterVarsity Press

Respondent: James Brownson, Western Theological Seminary

2016 Session 3—Theme: "Migration, Marginalization, and the Mission of God: Missional Hermeneutics in the Context of Human Displacement and Relocation"

Presider: Eunice McGarrahan, First Presbyterian Church, Colorado Springs

Bo H. Lim, Seattle Pacific University
"Towards a Theological Interpretation of Exile and Migration"

Gregory Perry, Covenant Theological Seminary
"Luke's Survey of Holy Places Outside 'the Land' in Stephen's
Speech: Hermeneutical Guidelines for Describing the Mobile
Dwelling Place and the People of God"

Respondent: Colin Yuckman, Duke University

**2017 Session 1—Roundtable Consultation: "Whither Missional
Hermeneutics?"**

Presider: John R. Franke, Second Presbyterian Church, Indianapolis

Panelists: George Hunsberger, Western Theological Seminary
James V. Brownson, Western Theological Seminary
Lois Barrett, Anabaptist Mennonite Biblical Seminary
Bo H. Lim, Seattle Pacific University
Andy Johnson, Nazarene Theological Seminary

**2017 Session 2—Roundtable Consultation: "Whither Missional
Hermeneutics?"**

Presider: Jim Brownson, Western Theological Seminary

Panelists: Michael Barram, Saint Mary's College of California
John R. Franke, Second Presbyterian Church, Indianapolis
Dennis R. Edwards, Sanctuary Covenant Church
Christina Busman Jost, Bethel University

2017 Session 3—Theme: "Navigating Citizenship"

Presider: Michael Barram, Saint Mary's College of California

Mark Glanville, Missional Training Center, Phoenix
"'Citizenship' and Inclusion in Deuteronomy and
in Contemporary Western Discourse"

Amanda Pittman, Abilene Christian University
"Shipwreck and Salvation: The Scope, Shape, and Social Implications of Paul's Confidence in God's Purposes in Acts 27:1–44"

Dennis Edwards, Sanctuary Covenant Church
"Citizens Worthy of the Gospel"

Julien C. H. Smith, Valparaiso University
"Philippians and the Challenge of Citizenship in
the Heavenly *Politeuma.*"

**2018 Session 1—Theme: Panel Review Discussion of *Henning Wroge-
mann's Intercultural Hermeneutics, Vol. 1: Intercultural Theology*
(IVP Academic, 2016)**
Presider: Colin Yuckman, Duke Divinity School

Panelists: Drew Hart, Messiah College
Lisa Bowens, Princeton Theology Seminary
Michael Barram, Saint Mary's College of California
Young Lee Hertig, Innovative Space for Asian American Christianity

**2018 Session 2—Theme: "American Politics and Missional Hermeneutics
in Interpreting the New Testament"**
Presider: Andy Johnson, Nazarene Theological Seminary

Mark Simon, Ridley College, Melbourne
"Power Games or Powerful Transformation? A Missional
Reading of Ephesians for Political Engagement"

Dean Flemming, MidAmerica Nazarene University
"Babylon Left Behind: Reading Revelation 17 and 18 Missionally
in Light of Ancient and Contemporary Political Contexts"

Michael Rhodes, Memphis Center for Urban Theological Studies
"Arranging the Chairs in the Beloved Community: The Politics,
Problems, and Prospects of Multi-Racial Congregations in
1 Corinthians and Today"

Sylvia Keesmaat, Toronto School of Theology, and Brian Walsh, University of Toronto
"Romans Disarmed: Homemaking in the 'Home' of the Brave"

2018 Session 3—Theme: "The Status and Direction of the Forum on Missional Hermeneutics" (A Workshop Meeting)

Presider: Michael Barram, Saint Mary's College of California

2019 Session 1—Theme: "Missional Hermeneutics in Contemporary Context: Missionally Located Interpretation of the Hebrew Scriptures / Old Testament"

Presider: Lisa Bowens, Princeton Theological Seminary

Boaz Johnson, North Park University
"A Dalit (Outcaste) Indian Interpretation of the Megillot: Ruth, Song of Songs, Ecclesiastes, Lamentations and Esther"

Chuck Pitts, Houston Graduate School of Theology
"Jeremiah and the Life of Shalom"

Len Firth, Ridley College, Melbourne, Australia
"I Will Gather the Nations: Reading the Prophet Zechariah from a Refugee Perspective"

Michael Rhodes, Memphis Center for Urban Theological Studies
"Becoming Just: The Deuteronomic Tithe Feast as Morally Transformative Practice"

Discussion: Reflecting on the Nature and Practice of Missional Hermeneutics

2019 Session 2—Theme: "Book Review Panel Discussion of Michael Barram's *Missional Economics: Biblical Justice and Christian Formation* (Eerdmans, 2018)"

Presider: Darrell Guder, Princeton Theological Seminary

Introduction: Michael Barram, Saint Mary's College of California

Panelists: Christina Busman Jost, Bethel University
Drew Hart, Messiah College
Colin Yuckman, Duke Divinity School
John R. Franke, Second Presbyterian Church

Respondent: Michael Barram, Saint Mary's College of California

2019 Session 3—Theme: "James Cone, Blackness, and Missional Hermeneutics"
Presider: Dennis Edwards, Northern Seminary

Mark Glanville, Grandview Calvary Church, Vancouver;
Missional Training Center, Phoenix
"Reading Scripture Missionally in Light of James Cone's Theology of the Cross"

Boaz Johnson, North Park University
"The Black Liberation Theology and Black Identity of James Cone and the Dalit Liberation Theology and Dalit Identity of James Massey"

Joseph W. Caldwell, Union University
"Reading Scripture while Reading Cone Reading Baldwin: A Theological Hermeneutical Lens on Biblical Suffering"

Conversation moderated by Drew Hart, Messiah College

2020 Session 1—*Session Theme:* Hermeneutical Approaches Informed by the Positionalities of Women in Dialogue with Missional Hermeneutics
Presider, Stina Busman Jost, Bethel University

Stina Busman Jost, Bethel University
"Pauses and Possibilities: Missional Theology in Dialogue with
Theologies Grounded in the Positionalities of Women"

Kirsteen Kim, Fuller Theological Seminary
"*Missio Dei* not *Missio Patri*: An Examination of the Patriarchal
Origins of Missional Theology and Suggestions for Trinitarian
Missional Hermeneutics"

Greg McKenzie, Lipscomb University
"Revisioning the 'Mission' of Missional Hermeneutics as
Solidarity: Womanist, Mujerista, and Feminist Contribu-
tions to a Postcolonialist Missiology"

Sarah Bixler, Eastern Mennonite University
"A Great Co-mission: Heeding Women's Problematization
of 'Teaching Them'"

Amanda Pittman, Abilene Christian University
"Navigating the Ambiguities: A Missional Reading of
the Women in Luke's Gospel"

2020 Session 2—Theme: Reparations / Reparational Ethics, the
Bible, and the *Missio Dei* (A joint session with the SBL Ethics
and Biblical Interpretation Section)

Presider, Kristopher Norris, Wesley Theological Seminary

Michael J. Rhodes, Union University
"The Jubilee Case for Reparations: Interpreting Scripture's
Jubilary Theology in the Aftermath of the Black Manifesto"

Michael Barram, Saint Mary's College of California
"Biblical Formation for Reparation: Missional and Moral Logics
for a More Just Future"

Matthew Schlimm, University of Dubuque Theological Seminary
"No Future Without Repentance: Pentateuchal Precedents for
Reparative Justice"

2020 Session 3—Theme: Interrogating the Terminology and Grammar
of "Missional" Hermeneutics

Presider, John Franke, Second Presbyterian Church, Indianapolis
Panelists: Michael Barram, Saint Mary's College of California
Dennis Edwards, North Park Theological Seminary
Stina Busman Jost, Bethel Seminary
Bo Lim, Seattle Pacific University
Lisa Bowens, Princeton Theological Seminary
John Franke, Second Presbyterian Church, Indianapolis

2021 Session 1—Theme: Book Review Panel: *Missional Theology:
An Introduction* (Baker Academic, 2020), by John R. Franke

Presider, Michael Barram, Saint Mary's College of California

Introduction, John R. Franke, Second Presbyterian Church,
Indianapolis

Panelists: Lalsangkima Pachuau, Asbury Theological Seminary
Kirsteen Kim, Fuller Theological Seminary
David Moe, Asbury Theological Seminary
Greg McKinzie, Lipscomb University

Respondent: John R. Franke, Second Presbyterian Church,
Indianapolis

2021 Session 2—Theme: Missional Hermeneutics and Whiteness

Panelists: Michael Barram, Saint Mary's College of California
Odell Horne Jr., Evangelical Theological Seminary (PA)
Mark Glanville, Regent College
Daniel White Hodge, North Park University
Drew Hart, Messiah College
Dennis Edwards, North Park Theological Seminary

2021 Session 3—Theme: Missional Hermeneutics Moving Forward:
A Visioning and Planning Session

Presider, Michael Barram, Saint Mary's College of California

Presider, John R. Franke, Second Presbyterian Church, Indianapolis

2022 Session 1—Theme: Missional Hermeneutics: An Interactive
Workshop Facilitated by Michael Barram

Presider, Michael Barram, Saint Mary's College of California

2022 Session 2—Theme: Missional Hermeneutics as an Interpretive
Posture: Conversational Reflections on Paul and His Legacy

Panelists: John R. Franke, Second Presbyterian Church,
Indianapolis
Lisa M. Bowens, Princeton Theological Seminary
Michael J. Gorman, Saint Mary's Seminary & University

2022 Session 3—Theme: The Forum on Missional Hermeneutics:
Steering Committee Meeting

Presider: Michael Barram, Saint Mary's College of California

2023 Session 1—Theme: "Missional Peacemaking: Engaging Polarization
in Ecclesial and Educational Contexts"

Presider, Julien Smith, Valparaiso University

Michael Barram, Saint Mary's College of California
"Are Peacemakers Really Blessed? Reading Jesus's Sermon on the
Mount Missionally in Polarized Contexts"

Gustaf W. Henriksson, Oslo University
"The Light of Love: Learning from Paul and Receptive Ecumen-
ism in the Walk towards Unity for the Sake of the World"

Ronald T. Michener, Evangelische Theologische Faculteit
"Humble Posturing for Missional Peacemaking in
the Church and Academy"

Sarah Bixler, Eastern Mennonite University, respondent

Eunice "Junior" McGarrahan, First Presbyterian Church,
Colorado Springs, respondent

**2023   Session 2—Theme: "Re-examining Acts 17:26 Missionally:
Interpretation and Implications"**
Dennis Edwards, North Park Theological Seminary, Presiding

Grant LeMarquand, Trinity School for Ministry
"African Readings of Paul's Preaching in Athens (Acts
17:16–34)"

Vince Bantu, Fuller Theological Seminary (Texas)
"Hermeneutic of Cultural Sanctification"

David Evans, Eastern Mennonite University, Respondent

Amanda Pittman, Abilene Christian University, Respondent

2023   Session 3—Theme: Steering Committee and Planning Meeting
Michael Barram, Saint Mary's College of California, Presiding

John R. Franke, Second Presbyterian Church,
Indianapolis, Presiding

Steering Committee Members of the Forum on Missional Hermeneutics

Michael Barram, Co-Chair	Darrell L. Guder	Michael J. Rhodes
John R. Franke, Co-Chair	George R. Hunsberger	Colin H. Yuckman
Lois Y. Barrett	Andy Johnson	
Lisa M. Bowens	Bo H. Lim	
Christina Busman	Andrew J. Mainiero	**Former Members:**
Kristin Caynor	Eunice McGarrahan	James V. Brownson
Dean Flemming	Greg McKenzie	Dennis R. Edwards
Mark R. Glanville	Chuck Pitts	Michael J. Gorman
Jeffrey P. Greenman	Amanda Jo Pittman	James C. Miller

Discussion Questions

Chapter 1

Why *Missional* Interpretation?

1. Barram and Franke note that traditionally, "mission" has thus been understood in terms of human activity—e.g., evangelism, outreach efforts, and the geographical expansion of Christianity. The authors argue, however, that "mission" is, first and foremost about God, and best understood in terms of biblical testimony to divine purposes—the *missio Dei*, or "mission of God"—and only then, derivatively, of human participation in those same divine purposes. By implication, any biblically faithful notion of "mission" involves what goes on *within* the Christian community (e.g., worship, formation, congregational budgets) no less than what happens *beyond* it (e.g., evangelism, social outreach, "missionary" efforts). Reflect on and discuss both the traditional view of mission and the reimagined understanding advocated in this book. How do you react to the shift from a traditional understanding of mission to a purposive one? How might this new approach to mission affect your own thinking about God? About Scripture? About the church and its calling?

2. *Liberating Scripture* argues that because mission is fundamentally about God and divine purposes, missional interpretation involves a posture of approaching Scripture in ways that emphasize those divine purposes—in light of who God is, what God cares about, and what God is doing in

173

and through creation. Reading the Bible "missionally" is thus *not* about searching for passages, for example, about evangelism or outreach beyond the Christian community (e.g., Matt 28:16–20), but rather about reading *every* scriptural text looking for indications of both divine purposiveness and formation for human participation within the *missio Dei*. How does this shift in perspective affect your own thinking about and understanding of Scripture? What new insights might familiar passages hold? How might this new way of approaching Scripture affect how you read and engage with less familiar texts?

Chapter 2

Missional Hermeneutics and Biblical Interpretation

1. Reflect on the three "lenses" through which all of us interpret Scripture, reviewing their characteristics and contributions. Were any of these interpretive lenses already familiar to you? What was new for you in this discussion of interpretation? Do you find yourself and/or your community of faith more drawn to or comfortable with one or two of the lenses than with another? Which of the lenses may need more conscious attention and emphasis in your own engagement with Scripture going forward?

2. Reflect seriously on the various aspects of your own personal social location. What facets of that location may be especially helpful as you begin to experiment with missional interpretation of Scripture? What facets of your social location may potentially hinder your efforts to engage more fully in missional interpretation and to participate more faithfully and holistically within divine purposes?

3. Reflect on the various aspects of the social location of your faith community. What facets of that location may hinder your collective ability to engage and participate more faithfully and holistically within divine purposes? Are there blind spots—e.g., socioculturally, politically, economically, theologically—that hinder the community's ability to recognize and follow the movement and intentions of God? Reflect and discuss—again and again!

4. Return again to the questions on pp. 48–49. Choose two or three for reflection and discussion.

Chapter 3

How We Shackle Scripture

1. Do any of the ways that as readers we tend to "shackle" Scripture (as discussed in this chapter) sound familiar to you? Do you recognize any of these tendencies in your own engagement with the Bible? Have you known others who tend to approach Scripture in one or more of these ways?

2. On p. 70, the authors note that "many readers *claim* to read Scripture *literally*, but when we ignore genre we end up reading not what the text actually says but rather what they assume it does." Do some reflection on this statement individually and with others.

3. In light of the discussion in chapter 3, reflect on the following quote on p. 72: "It is ironic, but nonetheless true: the Bible itself needs to be liberated from our tendencies to control it. Indeed, the more we learn to 'liberate' the Bible, the more fully we can experience the liberation it seeks to offer to us." Discuss.

Chapter 4

Toward a Vision of the *Missio Dei*

1. Have you ever thought about the differences between the eternal mission of God and the temporal mission of God? How does the idea that the mission of God never ends, ever after the consummation of all things, shape your understanding of the mission of God on earth?

2. Based on your reading of chapter 4, how would you describe the mission of God in your own words? What do you think of the term mission? Do you understand why some people believe it should be abandoned? What do you think?

Chapter 5

The Liberating Word

1. On p. 84 the authors write, "If our experience is anything close to typical, when most Christians hear the phrase 'the word of God,' they immediately think of the Bible—and only the Bible." Is this your experience? What do you think of when you hear the phrase "word of God"? Do you think of anything other than the Bible? What do you think of the idea of the threefold form of the word of God?

2. What do you think about the idea that divine self-revelation is God's accommodation to the limitations of finite human understanding? And if this is the case, what implications might there be for your own understanding of revelation and the Bible?

3. The authors suggest on p. 91 that the event of Pentecost and the subsequent history of Christianity points to "the infinite translatability of the gospel," leading to "fresh adaptations" of the gospel and the "irreducible plurality" of the Christian faith. What do you think of this idea? Does it make sense to you? Why or why not? How does it relate to your understanding of faith and the gospel?

4. What do you think of the idea of Christian pluralism? Do you see this as compromising Christian commitments? Why or why not? How might it invite a fresh understanding of the message of Jesus and the mission of God?

Chapter 6

Missional Hermeneutics and Theological Interpretation

1. The authors maintain that in the task of interpreting the Bible, it is important to distinguish between exegesis and hermeneutics. How do you understand exegesis and hermeneutics? How are they different from each other? Why are both necessary for a missional reading of Scripture?

2. The authors write on p. 110 "that no single human perspective, whether of an individual or a particular community, or a theological tradition, is adequate to do full justice to the truth of God's revelation in Christ." How

do you respond to this? Do you agree? Why or why not? What are the implications of this for your reading of the Bible?

3. On p. 113, the authors assert that theology is not a universal language. They conclude that theology "is always a particular interpretation of revelation, Scripture, and tradition that reflects the goals, aspirations, and beliefs of a particular people, a particular community. As such, theology cannot speak for all. When it insists on doing so, and when this insistence is coupled with cultural and societal power, it becomes oppressive to those who do not share its values and outlooks, leaving them painfully disenfranchised." What do you think of this statement? If it is true, how do our conceptions of theology need to change? What might an alternative approach look like in practice? How important do you think this is for the future of Christian witness?

4. On p. 114, the authors write that "the dominant theologies of North American history have contributed to the racism that permeates society." How do you respond to this statement? How might theology have contributed to our social situation? And how could and should the racism within our society be addressed by future theologies?

Chapter 7

The Practice of Missional Hermeneutics

1. As you reflect on what you have read in *Liberating Scripture*, are there ways in which you may already be experiencing even more of the liberating power of Scripture—particularly by approaching it from a "missional" perspective?

2. Were the reflections on Matt 18:21–35; Gen 38:1–30; and Lev 25 helpful to you, particularly as examples of a missional approach to Scripture? Following this book-length invitation to and proposal for missional hermeneutics, what biblical texts might you want to read—or *reread*— from this perspective?

3. Choose a scriptural text to explore, preferably one of approximately eight to twelve verses in length. (It is important to try, whenever possible, not to begin analyzing a text in the middle of a story, short paragraph, or thought unit. And it is equally important to avoid cutting a passage off

prematurely, in the middle of a sentence or thought. Try to choose a passage that "holds together" as a unit.) Then, select a few of the questions from each of the four groups of questions on pp. 143–45, which will encourage you to consider all three interpretive "lenses" in various ways), and begin experimenting with missional hermeneutics, discussing your reading of the passage with others!

Bibliography

Augustine. *On Christian Doctrine.* In *Nicene and Post-Nicene Fathers,* edited by Philip Schaff and translated by J. F. Shaw, 2:532–33. Peabody, MA: Hendrickson, 2004.

Barram, Michael. "The Bible, Mission, and Social Location." *Interpretation: A Journal of Bible and Theology* 61 (2007) 42–58.

———. "Economic and Social Reparations: The Jubilee as Biblical Formation for a More Just Future." *Word and World: Theology for Christian Ministry* 42 (2022) 77–86.

———. "'Fools for the Sake of Christ': Missional Hermeneutics and Praxis in the Corinthian Correspondence." *Missiology: An International Review* 43 (2015) 195–207.

———. *Missional Economics: Biblical Justice and Christian Formation.* Grand Rapids: Eerdmans, 2018.

———. "Missional Hermeneutics." In the *Handbook of Intercultural Theology and Missiology,* edited by Dorottya Nagy and John Flett. London: T. & T. Clark, forthcoming.

———. *Mission and Moral Reflection in Paul.* New York: Peter Lang, 2006.

———. "Reparational Reasoning: The Biblical Jubilee as Moral Formation for a More Just Future." In *Reparations and the Theological Disciplines: Prophetic Voices for Remembrance, Reckoning, and Repair,* edited by Michael Barram et al. Lanham, MD: Lexington, 2023.

Barth, Karl. *Church Dogmatics* 1/2. Edited by T. F. Torrance and G. E. Bromiley, and translated by G. E. Bromley. Edinburgh: T. & T. Clark, 1956.

Bauckham, Richard. *The Bible and Mission: Christian Witness in a Postmodern World.* Grand Rapids: Baker Academic, 2003.

Bevans, Stephen B., and Roger P. Schroeder. *Constants in Context: A Theology of Mission for Today.* Maryknoll, NY: Orbis, 2004.

"BISAM." International Association for Mission Studies, n.d. https://missionstudies.org/index.php/study-groups/bisam/.

Blauw, Johannes. *The Missionary Nature of the Church: A Survey of the Biblical Theology of Mission.* London: McGraw-Hill, 1962.

Bosch, David J. *Transforming Mission: Paradigm Shifts in Theology of Mission.* Maryknoll, NY: Orbis, 1992.

Brownson, James V. *Speaking the Truth in Love: New Testament Resources for a Missional Hermeneutic.* Harrisburg, PA: Trinity Press International, 1998.

Franke, John R., ed. *Ancient Christian Commentary: Joshua, Judges, Ruth, 1–2 Samuel.* Old Testament 4. Downers Grove, IL: InterVarsity, 2005.

———. *Missional Theology: An Introduction.* Grand Rapids: Eerdmans, 2020.

Friere, Paulo. *Pedagogy of the Oppressed.* 50th anniversary ed. Translated by Myra Bergman Ramos. Repr. New York: Bloomsbury, 2018.

Goheen, Michael W. *A Light to the Nations: The Missional Church and the Biblical Story.* Grand Rapids: Baker Academic, 2011.

Gorman, Michael J. *Becoming the Gospel: Paul, Participation, and Mission.* Grand Rapids: Eerdmans, 2015.

Grenz, Stanley J., and John R. Franke. *Beyond Foundationalism: Shaping Theology in a Postmodern Context.* Louisville, KY: Westminster John Knox, 2001.

Guder, Darrell L. *Called to Witness: Doing Missional Theology.* Grand Rapids: Eerdmans, 2015.

———. "Unlikely Ambassadors: Clay Jar Christians in God's Service: A Bible Study for the 214th General Assembly of the Presbyterian Church (USA)." Louisville: Office of the General Assembly, Presbyterian Church (USA), 2002.

Guder, Darrell L., et al, eds. *Missional Church: A Vision for the Sending of the Church in North America.* Grand Rapids: Eerdmans, 1998.

Gutiérrez, Gustavo. *A Theology of Liberation: History, Politics and Salvation.* Translated and edited by Sr. Caridad Inda and John Eagleson. Maryknoll, NY: Orbis, 1973.

Hahn, Ferdinand. *Mission in the New Testament.* Translated by Frank Clarke. London: SCM, 1965.

Hunsberger, George R. "Mapping the Missional Hermeneutics Conversation." In *Reading the Bible Missionally,* edited by Michael W. Goheen, 45–67. Grand Rapids: Eerdmans, 2016.

———. "Proposals for a Missional Hermeneutic: Mapping a Conversation." *Missiology: An International Review* 39 (2011) 309–21.

International Council on Biblical Inerrancy. "A Short Statement" and "The Chicago Statement on Biblical Inerrancy." 1978. https://www.etsjets.org/files/documents/Chicago_Statement.pdf.

Johnson, Elizabeth A. *Quest for the Living God: Mapping Frontiers in the Theology of God.* New York: Continuum, 2007.

Kwon, Duke L., and Gregory Thompson. *Reparations: A Christian Call for Repentance and Repair.* Grand Rapids: Brazos, 2021.

Legrand, Lucién. *Unity and Plurality: Mission in the Bible.* Maryknoll, NY: Orbis, 1990.

Mayo, Maria. *The Limits of Forgiveness: Case Studies in the Distortion of a Biblical Ideal.* Eugene, OR: Wipf & Stock, 2021.

McKenzie, Greg. "The Hermeneutics of Participation: Missional Interpretation of Scripture and Readerly Formation." Unpublished PhD diss., Fuller Theological Seminary, 2021.

———. "Missional Hermeneutics as Theological Interpretation." *Journal of Theological Interpretation* 11 (2017) 157–79.

Moltmann, Jürgen. *The Church in the Power of the Spirit.* Minneapolis: Fortress, 1993.

Newbigin, Lesslie. *The Gospel in a Pluralist Society.* Grand Rapids: Eerdmans, 1989.

Rhodes, Michael J. "From Here to Jubilee: Reading the Torah in Dialogue with Darity and Mullen's Case for Reparations." In *Reparations and the Theological Disciplines: Prophetic Voices for Remembrance, Reckoning, and Repair,* edited by Michael Barram et al., 43–61. Lanham, MD: Lexington, 2023.

Rohr, Richard. *Jesus' Plan for a New World: The Sermon on the Mount.* Cincinnati: St. Anthony Messenger, 1996.

Sanneh, Lamin. *Translating the Message: The Missionary Impact on Culture.* 2nd ed. Maryknoll, NY: Orbis, 2009.

Senior, Donald, and Carroll Stuhlmueller. *The Biblical Foundations for Mission.* Maryknoll, NY: Orbis, 1994.

Smith, Christian. *The Emergence of Liberation Theology: Radical Religion and Social Movement Theory.* Chicago: University of Chicago Press, 1991.

Thurman, Howard. *Jesus and the Disinherited.* Nashville: Abingdon, 1949.

Wright, Christopher J. H. *The Great Story and the Great Commission: Participating in the Biblical Drama of Mission.* Grand Rapids: Baker Academic, 2023.

———. *The Mission of God: Unlocking the Bible's Grand Narrative.* Downers Grove, IL: IVP Academic, 2006.

Subject and Name Index

Note: Page numbers followed by "n" refer to footnotes.

Scripture Index

Note: References followed by "n" refer to endnotes.

Made in the USA
Las Vegas, NV
19 March 2024

87404474R00125